The Allies
of
Humanity

◆

BOOK TWO

The Allies
of
Humanity

◆

BOOK TWO

Human Unity, Freedom
& The Hidden Reality of Contact

Marshall Vian Summers

AUTHOR OF
STEPS TO KNOWLEDGE: The Book of Inner Knowing
Winner of the Year 2000 Best Spiritual Book of the Year Award

THE ALLIES OF HUMANITY, BOOK TWO:
Human Unity, Freedom and the Hidden Reality of Contact

Edited by Darlene Mitchell
Book Design by Alan Bernhard, Boulder, CO
Cover Design by Reed N. Summers

ISBN: 978-1-884238-37-6 *THE ALLIES OF HUMANITY, BOOK TWO: Human Unity, Freedom and
the Hidden Reality of Contact*

Library of Congress Control Number: 2001130786

PUBLISHER'S CATALOGING-IN-PUBLICATION
(Provided by Quality Books, Inc.)

Summers, Marshall Vian.
    The allies of humanity, book two : human unity, freedom & the hidden
reality of contact / Marshall Vian Summers
    p. cm.
    LCCN 2001130786
    ISBN 978-1-884238-37-6

    1. Civilization—Extraterrestrial influences.
    2. Life on other planets.   3. Human-alien encounters.
    4. Spirituality.   I. Title.

BF2050.S86 2004   001.942
                                                        QB104-700339

Foreign translations and publishing inquiries are welcomed.
Because the Allies of Humanity have a worldwide message, New Knowledge Library is seeking
both publishers for foreign rights and/or readers who will translate the Allies Briefings. Already
international readers have taken up the banner to translate this vital message into French,
Spanish and Greek. If you as a reader feel called to translate *The Allies of Humanity Briefings*
into your native language so that others can learn the truth about the Intervention and
humanity's greatest threshold, please contact New Knowledge Library. If you can recommend
foreign publishers/translators, please do so.

ACKNOWLEDGMENTS
The book you hold in your hands is the product of the generous giving of others. Thank you
to those readers from around the world who answered the call and generously donated to
the production of this book. By helping us to disseminate this message worldwide, you are
supporting the grassroots movement to alert humanity to the great challenge that awaits us all.
May your gift in support of our freedom reverberate far into the future.

To receive information about The Society's audio recordings, educational programs and
contemplative services, please visit The Society on the worldwide web or write:

THE SOCIETY FOR THE GREATER COMMUNITY WAY OF KNOWLEDGE
P.O. Box 1724 • Boulder, CO 80306-1724 • (303) 938-8401
e-mail: society@greatercommunity.org   www.newmessage.org

Dedicated to

our allies beyond the world

who seek to share with us

their knowledge and wisdom of

life in the Universe so that humanity may

fulfill its destiny as a free race

in the Greater Community.

CONTENTS

The four fundamental questions about the
extraterrestrial presence in the world today:

What is happening?

Why is it happening?

What does it mean?

How can we prepare?

This Second Set of Briefings from the Allies of Humanity completes a crucial message regarding our vulnerability and potential within the Greater Community, the larger physical Universe in which we live. Communicated by a small group of extraterrestrial observers, the Briefings reveal the true nature and purpose of an extraterrestrial Intervention that has been underway in our world for quite some time. This group of observers represents the Allies of Humanity, an association of free races in the Universe who support the preservation of Knowledge and freedom throughout the Greater Community. The Allies distinguish themselves from the intervening forces that are here by maintaining their distance and not engaging directly with us. Instead, they offer us their wisdom about the realities of life in the Universe and a warning about the dangers and consequences of premature human/ET contact.

The arrival of *The Allies Briefings* was the result of a rare convergence of three powerful forces: the extraterrestrial, the Divine and the human. It was these essential forces that joined to enable *The Allies Briefings* to be delivered in a form and in a language that can be understood by everyday people. In this one book, each of these voices is represented: the extraterrestrial in the Allies Briefings, the Divine in the Teachers' Commentaries and the human in the Message from Marshall Vian Summers.

The story of how *The Allies of Humanity Briefings* came to be is as remarkable as the Briefings themselves. This story is presented here in an abbreviated form so that the reader can more fully understand the purpose of this great collaboration. This story describes the roles played by the Allies and the Angelic Presence in enabling this communication to happen, the inexplicable life of the man chosen to receive this message and the importance of the message itself.

Prior to receiving the first set of *The Allies Briefings*, Marshall Vian Summers had been working for over 20 years with an Angelic Presence that he had increasingly grown to trust and rely upon in his life and in his work. What began as an inner voice experience over time grew to be a potent relationship. This relationship prepared him for the magnitude of The Teaching in Greater Community Spirituality that he was destined to receive and to represent. During these years, he wrote some 20 volumes, all in a state of revelation. Many of these writings remain as yet unpublished and await funding. In total, they represent a new understanding of Self Knowledge, freedom and humanity's place within a Greater Community of intelligent life. His immense body of work stands as evidence of this human/Divine relationship and one day may be regarded as the first Theology of Contact.

Marshall's long collaborative relationship with this Angelic Presence set the stage for his encounter with the Allies of Humanity, who, as Marshall would discover later, were also students of these

Teachers of the Greater Community. It was these remarkable Teachers who entrusted Marshall with The Teaching in Greater Community Spirituality and opened a doorway to the realities of life in the Universe through contact with the Allies of Humanity.

In September 1996, the Teachers made possible the first contact between Marshall and the Allies. This contact occurred through what could be called a process of intuitive communication across a secure spiritual channel provided by the Teachers. As incredible as it may seem, this rare three-way communication enabled the Allies to speak directly to Marshall without the use of technology. And due to this secure channel provided by the Teachers, the Allies' communication could not be blocked or intercepted by the Intervention.

It wasn't until a whole year later, in November 1997, that Marshall received the first two Briefings for what would later become *THE ALLIES OF HUMANITY: Book One*. No one can fully account for this gap in time. However, it did give Marshall time to come to terms with this shift in his role from spiritual teacher to a messenger with a difficult message.

In the year following the delivery of the first two Briefings, Marshall struggled with the implications of what this initial information would mean both for himself and for the world.

Then, in October and December of 1998, the final four Briefings of Book One were provided.

While all of this was transpiring, we at New Knowledge Library were engaged in meeting the important challenge of publishing two of Marshall's major works, *GREATER COMMUNITY SPIRITUALITY: A New Revelation* and *STEPS TO KNOWLEDGE: The Book of Inner Knowing*, which was awarded The Year 2000 Book of the Year for Spirituality.

Also during this time, Marshall continued to write two more important books of this new revelation: LIVING THE WAY OF KNOWLEDGE and PREPARING FOR THE GREATER COMMUNITY, both of which still await publication. As a result, it was not until July 2000 that New Knowledge Library was able to produce an "underground" edition of THE ALLIES OF HUMANITY: Book One in order to begin to make the Allies' urgent message available.

It was in December 2000 that Marshall received the entire six briefings of THE ALLIES OF HUMANITY: Book Two within 24 hours. The Briefings were delivered very quickly for a reason. The Allies, threatened with being discovered by the Intervention, had to give their second set of Briefings to Marshall as quickly as possible before escaping to a distant location far from our Solar System. The Allies describe this situation in their Preface to the Second Set of Briefings, which is included in this volume.

Since that time, Marshall, along with the support of a growing number of courageous people, has endeavored to study and to bring The Allies of Humanity Briefings and message to the attention of as many people as possible. This ongoing work represents a vital mission and relies upon the contributions of readers everywhere in order to continue.

Whether or not any further Briefings will be sent here by the Allies is as yet uncertain. But what is certain is that the information contained in these two sets of Briefings provides the missing pieces to our understanding of the extraterrestrial presence in the world today and what we must do to begin to prepare. The Allies emphasize that these Briefings provide us everything that we need to know to begin this preparation with a clear understanding of our situation. We cannot afford to make the same mistakes that so many native peoples have made throughout the course of our own human history regarding their first encounters with explorers from the outside.

We at New Knowledge Library are proud to be able to present what may prove to be one of the most important documents ever published for the advancement, well-being and future of humanity. We recognize that some people may reject this information out of hand because of its possible association with "channeled" ET messages. However, given the high degree of his personal integrity and the extraordinary quality and relevance of his writings, Marshall's work stands apart. Truly, the revelations that have come to us through his work may ultimately prove to be as significant as other Divinely-inspired messages in the past that have impacted the course of human history.

We encourage you the reader to seriously explore the crucial message presented in all of these Briefings, in both Book One and Book Two, and to share this message with others. These Briefings represent a unique and greatly needed communication to all the people of our world at this critical turning point.

NEW KNOWLEDGE LIBRARY

WHO ARE
THE ALLIES OF HUMANITY?

The Allies serve humanity because they serve the reclamation and expression of Knowledge everywhere in the Greater Community. They represent the Wise in many worlds who support a greater purpose in life. Together they share a greater Knowledge and Wisdom that can be transferred across vast distances of space and across all the boundaries of race, culture, temperament and environment. Their wisdom is pervasive. Their skill is great. Their presence is hidden. They recognize you because they realize that you are an emerging race, emerging into a very difficult and competitive environment in the Greater Community.

◆

GREATER COMMUNITY SPIRITUALITY:
A New Revelation

We have come again to prepare you for more information that we would like to impart about the Greater Community presence in the world today and hopefully to address many of the questions that were generated by our first series of briefings. We understand from our own observations the degree to which humanity is unprepared for this great encounter that is taking place in your midst. There are many reasons for this, but the situation must change and we strongly recommend that you share this material with as many of your kind as you possibly can.

It is a difficult task to bear such a message and the greater reality that it represents. We hope and trust that you can find the support you will need to bring this into the world. There are many competing voices speaking to your world from the Greater Community, and there is much confusion. And along with this, there is human ambition. As a result, the situation has become very difficult. We have seen this elsewhere. It is not a unique problem for humankind.

The Greater Community presence is growing. Establishments are being built in your Solar System to provide a pathway for supplies and reinforcements. It is not a military buildup but more a network through which resources and equipment can be brought to your world. We see their establishments. You will not find them, for you cannot venture into space sufficiently yet, but a network is being built in this solar system to support the alien presence in your world today.

We are told by the Unseen Ones (the Angelic Presence) that there are those within the government of the American nation who are aware of the Intervention and are attempting to counteract it. But they do not have our counsel, and though they may recognize a certain degree of truth in the situation, they are without the necessary preparation. We are told that there are others within this government who have already united with the Intervention. And there are individuals in positions of economic power who have united with the Intervention.

It is still very early in the Intervention, and so there is much work that can be done. If people can make a connection with those in the government who oppose the Intervention, this would enable our voices to reach people in positions of power and authority. If this can be accomplished, it would be very helpful.

We have come to realize that our presence in your solar system must soon come to an end and that we are being forced to relocate beyond the reach of this solar system at a fair distance from it. As a result, our opportunities as observers will come to an end, for we will not be in a position to witness these things firsthand. Yet we can continue our counsel regarding the realities of life in the Universe. And we can maintain our link with our messenger. Our situation is becoming precarious, and we must soon withdraw, but before we do this, we want to impart to you more information. We must be careful not to present information that would only arouse idle speculation. That is the danger of presenting too many details. Here people lose their perspective of the overall situation and become fascinated or intrigued with certain things we might speak of regarding the nature of interactions between intelligent life in the Universe.

Once you have the proper perspective and understanding, and once you have a certain grasp of the realities of life in the Universe which will affect you directly, then you will not need our counsel as much. Then you will understand the Intervention enough to begin the process of counteracting it.

We must now withdraw and send our future communications from a much greater distance. There are many questions that we can answer, and there are some questions we cannot answer. Yet we do fully understand the great challenge facing humanity today and how the Intervention will be attempted. This we can address from our own experience and from our observations of life in the Universe.

It is true that if you have not yet encountered the realities of life in the Universe, you will tend to think that your values and your understanding are universal. You will think that life will revolve around you. And you will think that when the visitation occurs, somehow it must be for your benefit. These are common assumptions amongst emerging races such as your own. You will have to learn to overcome these assumptions to the best of your ability and to reach out to those who can hear our message at this time. We cannot ask for more than this.

As a result of our first set of briefings being presented in the form of a book, we became endangered and are now forced to withdraw, for there has begun a great search of the Solar System for us by your adversaries. Our hiding place now is no longer secure. A search is now underway for us, and even our escape will be difficult. We will be pursued. That is why we must now withdraw.

We will speak in these briefings a little more about our races though we will not give our names because certainly anything we provide to you will fall into the hands of your adversaries. Should they discover or even guess our origins, it would be very, very hazardous for our own home worlds.

With time and understanding, you will know why we have been sent. And you will know why we must now withdraw and find safe shelter further abroad. We do this without abandoning our mission, but only to place ourselves in a position where the mission can be furthered. Marshall, our messenger, is the link. We are not communicating to anyone else in the world.

...*O*ver twelve years ago, a group of
individuals from several different worlds
gathered at a discreet location in our
Solar System near the Earth for the
purpose of observing the alien Intervention that is occurring in our world. From
their hidden vantage point, they were
able to determine the identity, organization and intentions of those visiting our
world and monitor the visitors' activities.

This group of observers call themselves
the "Allies of Humanity."

This is their second report.

The
Briefings

◆

The Universe Into Which You are Emerging

We give greetings. We are very pleased to have this opportunity to speak with you once again and to provide the information that we are about to impart. We understand that our first series of commentaries has generated much interest, many questions and perhaps some confusion as well. We hope in this second volume, then, to provide more insight; to address some of these questions, if they can be answered; and to provide for you a window into the greater Universe in which you live so that you may see beyond the confines of your own world into the reality of life in the Greater Community. This is a necessary part of your education now, for your world is emerging into a Greater Community of intelligent life, a Greater Community in which you have always lived.

We have been sent to provide a series of briefings to help prepare humanity for this great threshold. Included in these briefings are our observations of the extraterrestrial Intervention that is occurring in the world today, why this Intervention is occurring, how it is being carried out and how it can be offset for your own well-being. This requires that you learn about life in the Greater Community so that you may become properly oriented to this new and far greater reality into which you are emerging.

Your ability to recognize the truth of what we are about to impart is absolutely fundamental for your survival, for your advancement, and indeed, for the preservation of the very freedoms that you hold most dear. For the Greater Community into which you are emerging is perhaps far different from what you may have thought before.

We have been sent to represent the allies of humanity. We are their representatives. We are not in your world, but have been observing your world from a hidden location nearby. We have not come to establish ourselves here, to build relations with the human family or to establish an economic or political liaison with your governments. We have come instead with a very simple mission. Our mission is to observe the extraterrestrial Intervention that is occurring in your world today and, given the opportunity to do so, provide the perspective that you will need to understand and to offset this Intervention and to prepare for the realities of life in the Universe.

The extraterrestrial intervention is not a mystery. It is a demonstration of nature.

Our first series of briefings provided a general view of the Intervention, how it is being carried out and what people must come to understand in order to avoid its influence and its persuasion and to recognize its reality. And yet there are more things that you must learn regarding this in order to gain the eyes to see and to understand these things for yourself. Though this may all seem strange and new to you, it is but another demonstration of nature, nature that you understand and comprehend within your own realm.

Nearly everything we are about to impart to you and that we have imparted already can be understood from your experience of nature. That is why the extraterrestrial Intervention is not a mystery. It is a demonstration of nature. Its difficulty, however, is that it casts you in a different role than you are used to. For you are used to being pre-eminent in your own world. You are used to feeling that you have the great evolutionary advantage within your own realm. But within the Greater Community, you do not have this pre-eminence or this advantage. Therefore, you must gain greater skill and a greater cooperation amongst yourselves.

> It is perhaps only the overshadowing of the Greater Community and the difficulties that it will confront you with that will enable humanity to unite and to find its common ground.

This is both a great difficulty and a great opportunity for your race, for it is perhaps only the overshadowing of the Greater Community and the difficulties that it will confront you with that will enable humanity to unite and to find its common ground. Whether this can be accomplished remains to be seen. But the challenge is upon you and that challenge confronts the life and the future of every person living in the world today.

At one moment, this may seem strange and incomprehensible, and yet in the next moment, you can understand that this is nature being carried out. You possess an environment and resources that are valued by others who seek to use and to have these things for themselves. It is your environment that they want. It is your help that they need. They do not seek to destroy you but to have you become part of their Collective in service to them.

This must be said many times in many different ways so that you can gain a very clear understanding. As we have said, this is not a mystery. It is but a presentation of your life in the Greater Community. It is the reality of nature, which you yourself can understand. Yet you are in a different position now, and this requires strength, discernment and human cooperation and a certain kind of sobriety regarding your understanding of the nature of life in the Universe.

There are great forces for good in the Universe, forces that work on behalf of individual freedom and the integrity of all life.

In this, our second set of briefings, we wish to give you a greater understanding and a greater vision of what life is really like in the Universe around you. It is not merely a matter of perspective. Our range of experience in these matters is very great amongst us. We have our own unique perspectives, but there are certain realities that are obvious to us, for we are in a position to see them and recognize them. We have lived through the opportunities and the difficulties of these realities—all things that you have yet to experience for yourselves. And yet your allies abroad wish to save you from the great risks that you now face, the risks of emerging into the Greater Community. They wish to show you your need to preserve your freedom and your integrity as a race as you undergo this difficult and prolonged transition.

This is the greatest challenge that any race in the Universe will ever face, and its consequences will be lasting and far reaching. And yet there are great forces for good in the Universe, forces that work on behalf of individual freedom and the integrity of all life, forces that seek to nurture and to keep alive the greater spiritual Knowledge that resides as a potential within all sentient beings. Your allies represent but a small expression of this greater force. For wherever there is life, there is the integrity of this spiritual Knowledge. It is not merely information; it is a living "Presence." We wish to demonstrate the reality and the meaning of this Knowledge and why it is so very fundamental to your success in healing the wounds of your world and in meeting the one great challenge that can unite and uplift humanity.

The Universe is full of life. But the Universe is immense. And intelligent life living in the physical manifestation is scattered about a great and vast arena. It is concentrated in some places more than others. In some ways, this resembles the maps of your countries, where there are large areas where many human people are congregated, and there are areas where very few people live at all. Between these areas of great congregation in the Universe, there are trade routes, great roads that are heavily traveled. In sparsely populated areas, there are very few routes, many of which are rarely if ever traveled.

We want to give you this analogy of the dispersal of intelligent life in this Galaxy. We have never ventured beyond the Galaxy, so we cannot speak of the other possibilities. Yet within this Galaxy alone, there is such a diversity of life. We ourselves have only seen a very, very small part of it, for the Galaxy is very great.

Your world exists in an area of congregation, an area that has many inhabited worlds. You do not see this within your own Solar System, but beyond your Solar System, this is most certainly true. You do not live in a sparsely populated part of the Universe. You do not live in a region that is uncharted and unknown to others. This gives you certain disadvantages because your world is being scrutinized by many powerful forces. They are seeking an Intervention now because humanity has reached a point in its development where it has built an infrastructure that other races believe they can use for themselves. This is why the Intervention did not happen at an earlier time. It was allowed for

> You do not live in a sparsely populated part of the Universe. You do not live in a region that is uncharted and unknown to others.

humanity to discover the resources and build the infrastructure first. In other words, you did the work for those who believe that you will serve them in the future.

Therefore, you do not live in a distant and remote part of the Galaxy. This you must understand. Travel in space occurs along certain routes or avenues, just like in your world. Certain roads are heavily traveled; others are rarely traveled. Your world exists in an area of considerable travel, which means there are many races using these routes for commerce and trade.

> Within this region, there are several emerging races such as your own, all being carefully watched by others.

Within this region, there are several emerging races such as your own, all being carefully watched by others.

As we have said in our previous discourses, the Greater Community into which you are emerging is a competitive environment on a scale you can hardly imagine. Trade and competition for resources, for alliances and for worlds that have strategic value, are considerable. And yet, the situation is far more complex than it might seem at first. Conquest of other lands is not tolerated in well-inhabited areas. Because of the competitive environment, there are restraints. Rules have been established over a long period of time regarding how trade will be conducted and what rules and guidelines will be followed. The violation of these rules brings retribution from one's adversaries and competitors, and so there is a system of checks and balances. This system is generally obeyed, but as is so often the case, exceptions are sought in many different ways. It is important for you to know that it is not allowed for your world to be invaded, militarily speaking. The forces that are intervening in your world are not strong military forces. They are great commercial forces. We call them "Collectives." And you will have an opportunity in this second set of discourses to learn more about their nature and structure.

In order for economic powers to gain access to your world and to gain control of your world, they must use more subtle means—means of persuasion, means of inducement. They must make it appear that you want them to be here, to welcome them, to want what they have to offer, to seek their assistance and their initial offerings. They want you to believe that you need them and that without them, you cannot succeed. In this way, they satisfy the restraints that are placed upon them. In this way, they can gain control of your world according to the rules that have been established.

> The forces that are intervening in your world are not strong military forces. They are great commercial forces.

The persuasion and the inducement that will be placed upon your world are very powerful and very compelling. Many people, by their own inclinations and by the weakness of their own position in life, will be very attracted to this persuasion. And yet, it is but a deception. It is a seduction. Then seemingly with humanity's general approval, the Intervention can begin and can be fulfilled without violating any restrictions that prevent invasion, conquest, and so forth.

If your world existed in a very remote or uncharted area, an area where these kinds of rules of trade and conduct had not been established, then military conquest would be attempted, for there would be nothing to prevent it from happening. But those who seek to take advantage of this world do not engage in military conquest. They do not need to. It is not their emphasis. It is not their purpose. They are not organized to do this.

They rely upon your weakness, as you must learn to rely upon your strength. They rely upon your lack of confidence in the human spirit, as you must learn to rely upon this spirit within yourselves. Their presence here holds great dangers for humanity and great opportunities if humanity can respond responsibly and wisely.

Therefore, it is our desire and our intention to help you in this preparation by giving you a perspective and an orientation to the reality that you are now facing and that you will face continuously from this time forward. For there is no returning to your former isolated state. Now you must learn to value and to protect your freedom, to consolidate your freedom and to build your freedom in an environment where that freedom will be under constant challenge. Only a world that is strong and united and wise in its dealings with the Greater Community can maintain its autonomy and remain free in the Universe. This is true of all free worlds, whether they exist in areas of congregation or whether they exist in remote areas that are rarely visited.

> Only a world that is strong and united and wise in its dealings with the Greater Community can maintain its autonomy and remain free in the Universe.

This is nature. Because other worlds have created greater levels of technology does not change the realities of life. It only makes the interactions between worlds more complicated and often more difficult to discern. It is easier to recognize a military confrontation than it is to recognize the hidden intent of those who come seeking to bear gifts and answers and the marvels of technology.

Humanity is without education regarding the Greater Community. And that is why you are so vulnerable. Humanity is divided amongst its nations and its cultures. And that is why you are so vulnerable. Your dispositions and your religious beliefs cannot prepare you adequately for what faces you now.

In the Greater Community, there are many races who have achieved very high levels of maturity in their spiritual understanding and have achieved a state of freedom that humanity has not yet come even close to achieving. Unlike those who are visiting you, these societies do not involve themselves in interplanetary trade to a very great degree, if at all. They are not involved in exploration. They are not resource explorers. They do not seek to gain alliances for political and economic advantage, except in certain situations for their own defense. They do not exploit other worlds. They do not seek to seduce young races who are emerging into the Greater Community. They do not engage in war. They are not part of Collectives.

Humanity is without education regarding the Greater Community. And that is why you are so vulnerable.

Your allies, whom we represent, demonstrate this establishment, the establishment of free races. This freedom is very difficult to achieve and to maintain in the Universe. To function successfully in the Greater Community, you must be self-sufficient. You must be united. And you must be very discreet. Do you see these qualities demonstrated in the human family at this time? Are they demonstrated within you and in your relationships? We are imparting to you a greater Wisdom, a Wisdom that has been difficult for us to achieve, that we have achieved at great cost. Our ability to be here to assist humanity is a demonstration of this achievement. For unlike those intervening in your world at this time, we seek only to observe and to advise. Once our transmissions are complete, we will have to withdraw for our own safety. For we are here without any official permission from trading authorities, overseeing organizations, any-

To function successfully in the Greater Community, you must be self-sufficient. You must be united. And you must be very discreet.

thing like this. If those who are intervening in your world were to discover us, we would surely perish.

Unlike those intervening in your world at this time, we seek only to observe and to advise.

With the presentation of our first set of briefings, our own safety now is imperiled. Those races who are intervening in your world have already begun a search of your Solar System for us. Therefore, we must impart this information and then withdraw to a point far beyond your world, to a place where we can no longer observe the Intervention directly. That is why we must give this information to you *now*. That is why you must seek to learn it and to use it to the very best of your ability. For once we depart, there can be no further direct assistance to you.

That is why we give these briefings the greatest importance. That is why you must receive them and recognize them to be such. We will provide to you what you need to know regarding the nature of the Collectives, how they function, why they are here and what they are doing in the world. We will give you an overview of the realities of intelligent life in the Universe and how interactions actually do occur. We shall give you a perspective on the strategic importance of your world and where it stands in relation to other inhabited worlds in your proximity. We shall also speak of the greater Spiritual Powers that exist in the Universe and within the human family.

Your isolation is now over. You will never have it again.

Your isolation is now over. You will never have it again in the ways that you have known it previously. Therefore, listen carefully to all the things we are about to tell you.

Why the Intervention is Occurring

You may well ask at the outset, "Why is our world being visited? Why is there an Intervention?" There are several answers to these fundamental questions, some of which are obvious, and some are not.

Obviously, you live in a beautiful world with great biological diversity. It is a world that has not been destroyed through exploitation, though it is in danger of being so. It is a world that contains immense biological resources, life-giving resources, resources that are rare and difficult to find in a Greater Community of barren worlds. You, of course, do not yet realize the value of your own world. Having never lived abroad, you cannot yet appreciate the marvel of the world that you live in and why it is so valuable to others. But consider this: You live in a world with a remarkably temperate environment and tremendous biological beauty and diversity. You live in a world that has enormous water resources. You live in a world that has large tracts of habitable land for those races that can breathe your atmosphere. You have a world now that has a human presence and infrastructure that can be incorporated into foreign technologies. You belong to a race of people which is intelligent, although superstitious and ignorant of life in the Universe, thus making you malleable and susceptible to persuasion and inducement. You live in a virtual paradise. This is how your world is perceived.

When we first came to your world and observed it from a close proximity, we were amazed. It is far more beautiful and rich than we had imagined. Though we have never been on the surface of your world, we can see even from our vantage point what a glorious place it must be. We have seen interventions such as the one occurring in your world happening in worlds of far less value and merit. So, certainly your world is like a prize. The question is whether you will defend it, protect it and maintain it. If you do not, others will surely take it from you. Have you not already seen this in the history of your own world when tribes and indigenous peoples were overcome by foreign powers seeking advantage, and how the great wealth that these indigenous peoples possessed, even unknown to them, made their land and their world so valuable to others? Have you not seen this? Has this not been demonstrated in your world countless times? It is being so demonstrated even at this moment.

Now *you* are the indigenous peoples. And powerful, intervening forces are coming into your world seeking to establish themselves through subtle means, seeking to unite with humanity in spirit and in flesh, seeking to gain a foundation here from which they can establish their own authority and

> When we first came to your world and observed it from a close proximity, we were amazed. It is far more beautiful and rich than we had imagined.

> Your world is like a prize. The question is whether you will defend it, protect it and maintain it.

pre-eminence. Your world is so attractive, surely you can see that such an Intervention can occur if you think about it.

To the Collectives, who live mostly in technological environments, such a world is grand, spectacular and useful. Yet they are not driven by an artistic appreciation of your world. They are driven by the need for your world's resources. They see it as a prize, the best amongst many. They are surveying it even at this moment.

The advent of nuclear weapons in your world triggered the Intervention to go into its mature phase, for they realize that should you become stronger and have greater technological power, then the Intervention would be more difficult to achieve. They would have you believe that they are intervening to save you from your own self-destruction, but really they are seeking to intervene before the situation becomes too difficult. You have become powerful, but not yet powerful enough. They see your world's environment being destroyed, and they feel they cannot wait.

> The advent of nuclear weapons in your world triggered the Intervention to go into its mature phase.

These are perhaps the obvious reasons why your world is undergoing an Intervention. But what about the reasons that are not so obvious? Let us speak of these now.

Unknown to all but a few individuals in the world today, there are important secret depositories in your world, for your world has been used by even gracious societies to hide things of value deep within it. For millennia your world has been a safe haven for the storage of sacred and powerful items. There are some in the hierarchy of the Collectives who know of

> For millennia your world has been a safe haven for the storage of sacred and powerful items.

this. And that is why they give your world special importance. That is why they seek to use individuals in your world who have psychic abilities in order to gain access to those individuals who have an intrinsic knowledge of these important hidden treasures.

After all, your world, with its vast biological resources, is an exquisite place to hide things, small things, things that can be buried deep underground in places that would be very difficult to discover. And because native peoples were superstitious and have sparsely populated the earth for so long, many things of value have been stored here.

If you were to discover these things, well, perhaps they would seem of little value or use to you, for you have not the skill or the Knowledge to use them. But should they be discovered by you, this would make you extremely vulnerable in the Greater Community, for in one moment, you would have something that so many others would want. You would not have the skill or the means to protect what you had just discovered, and it would bring tremendous attention to your world, attention that you would not want.

It is true that humanity has been visited for a very long time. But there has never been an Intervention of this magnitude or this nature before.

This is why the Wise remain hidden in the Universe. This is why objects of power, even Wisdom itself, must be protected and guarded. It is the same in your world, surely. The Wisest are the most hidden. Those who have the greatest Knowledge are the hardest to find, except by those who are meant to find them.

Some of these depositories have been destroyed through the natural cycles of your earth's evolution. They have been destroyed through natural events. But some still exist. And because the Intervention is under way, those who have stored these things long ago cannot return for their own safety.

This is why it is true that humanity has been visited for a very long time. But there has never been an Intervention of this magnitude or this nature before. This may be confusing to some people, for they think that the Intervention is but another expression of an ongoing visitation and an ongoing alien presence in the world, but it is not really true. You do not yet have the skill to discern friend from foe, your allies from your adversaries, except through demonstration, and even here it would take a deeper insight to make this determination. Some people will think that we are humanity's adversaries and that those intervening are humanity's allies. This is so obviously untrue, but it is not obvious to you. For you are without Wisdom and awareness in these matters, and that is why we have come.

Your world contains, then, great treasures— great treasures in its biological diversity, in its water resources, in its temperate environment and in its hidden treasures. Yet there is another reason that the world is valuable. This would not be obvious to you, for you could not recognize this from your vantage point. And that is that the world is in a strategic position that is valuable to other races.

The world is in a strategic position that is valuable to other races.

To understand this, you would have to have an overview of competition between Collectives and the economic and political establishments in the region in which you live. There are many participants. There are conflicts, though war rarely exerts itself. Competition is carried out in more subtle and ingenious means, for technology can be shared, copied and purchased. It is power in the

Mental Environment, the power of persuasion and the power of insight, that holds the greatest advantage here. Humanity does not yet realize this, for it is still brutish in the exertion of its powers. But your education about the Greater Community must begin at some time. And surely this is the time!

The Intervention has many faces.

Your world's strategic position adds to its importance. There are several Collectives competing for pre-eminence in your world. They are competing with one another, though they are not at war. We are certain that you can think of examples of this within your own world. For example, many nations in your world could compete for the riches of a poorer country. Such competition is occurring now, and that is why the Intervention has many faces. That is why you will see many different kinds of craft hovering above your lands. You will encounter different races of beings, and it will be very confusing, and you will think, "Some are good, and some are bad. Some are here to help, and some maybe are not here to help." But you are only guessing. And it is only your hopeful expectations that would encourage you to think that anyone who is on the surface of your world is here for your good.

Your allies will not intrude. Your allies will not seek to manipulate you or give you power that you cannot yet assume or give you technologies that you cannot yet use constructively. Your allies do not seek to conquer you or to make you part of their associations.

Before you can advance in the Greater Community, first you must survive. And to survive, you must unite and protect your world from interventions such as is occurring here now. If you can secure your freedom, then Intervention will be very difficult to achieve, by legal means, at least. And you will have to become a power to be reckoned with, rather than a feeble race that is stewarding a beautiful planet.

We believe in the great truth and power that exist in the human heart, or we would not have made the long journey to come here, or placed ourselves at such great risk to spend these years observing the Intervention and its activities. Your allies believe in the promise of humanity.

However, such respect you will find rare in the Greater Community. For as is true in so many places, your value and your worth will be determined by what you own, what you can trade, what you can sell, what you can surrender. This is life. This is nature. Technology does not change this. You must learn this. If you believe that technology is your salvation, you will be saved for another race who is technologically superior to you.

> You will have to become a power to be reckoned with, rather than a feeble race that is stewarding a beautiful planet.

Please hear our words here. We speak from great experience. We cannot prove these things to you until you can see them yourself. And when you see them yourself, it will be so obvious! The Intervention is so obvious! But who can see it? From your vantage point, it is far more difficult to recognize. And until you can have a Greater Community education and perspective, until you learn about the realities of the Greater Community, how can you possibly understand? Your heart will know, but can you listen?

> If you believe that technology is your salvation, you will be saved for another race who is technologically superior to you.

People want a happy outcome. People want to avoid conflict and challenge. People do not want to change, necessarily. Yet that is not what life brings.

Humanity must become far stronger than it is

today. Human freedom must be the rallying cry. So when you ask, "Why our world?" you must recognize these things that we have mentioned. What is obvious you will be able to see. What is not obvious you will not be able to see, but you can still understand. You may choose, of course, to distrust our words. You may believe that it is impossible that we could communicate to you in this way. You may doubt the whole process by which we communicate. You may cast away our counsel. We understand. But you must follow the Wisdom that lives within you to really know and if you really know, then you will know that we are being true with you.

This is where the real proof will occur. If you seek a proof in demonstration only, well, you can be persuaded of many things. But only Knowledge within you can be persuaded by the truth itself. It cannot be deceived. This is your strongest and greatest hope. This is the greatest power in the Universe, and your visitors do not use it. This is the key. Learn The Way of Knowledge and you will have the key. If you want things to be shown to you, well, you will be led astray. You will be persuaded by other powers. You will follow what you want instead of what you truly know. The world will be given away. And the occupation will become complete.

> You live at a critical moment, perhaps the greatest moment in your world's history.

You live at a critical moment, perhaps the greatest moment in your world's history. You have come at a great time. Is this an accident? Is it a mistake? Or was it meant to be this way? You who may be unsettled in your life, seeking a greater reality and a greater meaning, surely you must consider this. You are the indigenous peoples of a world that is being visited for the purpose of conquest and domination. How will you respond?

The choice is yours. We can only advise. No one in the Greater

Community is going to come and rescue you. The Wise do not do that. Perhaps you question this and say, "Why not?" You must trust us in this matter because should we intervene in a military fashion, should we gather the strength to do that, our worlds would be jeopardized. We would be functioning outside our jurisdiction, violating the rules of conduct of that jurisdiction. Can you see this?

Even so, if humanity is to become strong and independent in the Universe, it must establish its own strength and independence. It cannot be rescued. What is confronting you is the reality of life in the Universe. It is not an evil power. It is not a sinister force. It is just the strong taking advantage of the weak, if it can. That is nature. That is life. Until you reach a greater spiritual understanding, an understanding of Knowledge, then that is the life that is real. Knowledge is as rare in the Universe as it is within your own world.

> No one in the Greater Community is going to come and rescue you. The Wise do not do that.

Many people place all their hope on being saved by a greater race. How will they know their allies from their adversaries? They are but ripe for the Intervention. They will seek to unite with the Intervention, believing it will save humanity from itself, believing what your visitors themselves believe, for they are convinced that humanity is far too unruly, disorganized and unworthy even to live in such a valuable place.

You cannot have a fanciful, romantic view of life in the Universe if you are to understand it and prepare for it accordingly. You must have wisdom and sobriety. You must be without self-deception in this matter. You are living in an environment of tremendous persuasion, not only persuasion between people but persuasion from

> What is confronting you is the reality of life in the Universe.

forces in the Greater Community that are in your midst. How will you overcome and offset this influence in your life? We must be emphatic and repetitive in what we are emphasizing because we want to assist you in overcoming these influences that would keep you in a state of confusion or ambivalence regarding the very forces that are threatening your well-being at this time.

You cannot have a fanciful, romantic view of life in the Universe if you are to understand it and prepare for it accordingly.

You have never been in a situation like this before. Certainly you have never faced an Intervention of this magnitude. People will deny its existence. They will laugh at it. They will scorn it. They do not want it to be true. They do not want it to be real. But that does not change the reality.

Since our first set of briefings, we understand that many people have asked about our names and our identities, where we have come from, and so forth, as if they must know these things in order to trust our words. But we cannot impart them, for we must remain hidden or we will be in great danger, and your allies who have sent us to be near the world will be in great danger as well.

It is not information you need as much as perspective. If you cannot see the situation clearly, what good is having more information?

The trust must come from a deeper understanding. It is not information you need as much as perspective. If you cannot see the situation clearly, what good is having more information? If you cannot know the truth in your own heart, what will the information provide for you? You need a little information. You need a lot of perspective. And you need a lot of courage.

Why is your world being visited? Why is there an Intervention? Think of these things, and you will see clearly. It is so obvious.

The Influence Upon Humanity

I t is vital for us to talk now about the nature of the inducement that is being placed upon humanity. Because this is an Intervention and not a visitation and because its overall aim and goal is domination of your world and the subjugation of the human race, the methods that will be employed will be used to encourage, to induce and to seduce humanity into a cooperative, subservient role to your visitors. Because your visitors are not allowed to invade this world outright, they must use these methods. Because there is more than one Collective functioning in the world seeking to attain this goal, they will all use these methods. In this, Collectives operate in much the same way.

Because they do not venture into uncharted or distant territories, the Collectives must maintain their focus where they have a concentration of power and where their organization can function effectively. In this, they have become quite adept in using the powers of persuasion. Their primary focus beyond their normal avenues of trade and commerce is to gain access to emerging worlds such as yours and to new mineral and biological discoveries in the regions in which they are dominant. In most regions, Collectives are

prevented from having a military presence beyond their own security forces. As a result, they must engage in more subtle and more
time-consuming activities. And yet this is seen by them as appropriate here because they want humanity's cooperation. They cannot
function in the world without your help. They cannot breathe your
atmosphere. They cannot gain access to your resources. They
cannot live upon the surface of your world effectively, and so in
order to take full advantage of the resources of your world and the
strategic position of your world, they must have human assistance.

> The Intervention does not want to risk a human revolution in the future. Such revolutions have happened before.

Indeed, beyond this, the Collectives that are
functioning in the world today want to add a human
component to their collective community and mentality. It is not simply that they want you to be a work
force for them; they want you to become a part of
them. This adds to their collective strength and will
minimize any resistance in the future that humanity
might mount for its own sake. This is why there is such
a great investment of time and energy in gaining human allegiance,
in bonding with humanity through interbreeding and in establishing
a deep and pervasive association with the human family.

This world is so valuable that the Intervention does not want
to risk a human revolution in the future. Such revolutions have
happened before. We can attest to this from our own experience.
We are the product of such revolutions in our own worlds. Though
our circumstances were quite different from yours, the nature of the
Intervention and the methods employed were actually quite similar.
This is why we can speak with authority on this subject.

The inducements that will be brought to bear will be varied,
depending on who is being reached and for what purpose. For indi-

viduals who are deemed receptive and cooperative in the halls of government, the inducement will be the promise of greater power and technology. Humanity is in a very vulnerable position in this sense because its belief in technology and its hope that technology will solve all of its problems are very, very strong. This of course has been supported by the Intervention because this is one of the primary avenues in which humanity will likely become dependent on the Intervention itself.

To those in the corridors of power in your governments, those individuals who are deemed receptive and cooperative, the promise of greater technology and even world dominion will be presented. This can be presented either through the Mental Environment as ideas sent into the minds of these individuals, or, as has already occurred, there may be face-to-face encounters with the visitors themselves.

> For individuals who are deemed receptive and cooperative in the halls of government, the inducement will be the promise of greater power and technology.

And what will they offer humanity? They will offer humanity some of their basic technology, certainly nothing that they consider to be advanced, unique, secret or sacred to them—basic propulsion in space, basic use of electronic energy, methodologies of production. They will not teach power in the Mental Environment, for they do not want humanity to have this power unless it is completely controlled and directed by the visitors themselves.

And who in your corridors of power could resist such a temptation? Many will succumb. They will see in these offerings wealth, power, control, domination and enormous advantage over their fellow humans and over other nations with whom they are competing directly. Only those individuals whose Knowledge is strong will be able to recognize the deception and resist the temptation presented in these inducements

People in positions of great economic power and wealth, if they are deemed cooperative and receptive, will be reached as well.

And again, who amongst them can resist such a temptation, such a promise of wealth, power and control? And yet these inducements are but a deception—a means of engaging other people in the activities of the Collective, a means of establishing a strong liaison.

> Who in your corridors of power could resist such a temptation?

Those people who are contacted, those individuals who fall prey to this deception, will not understand the real meaning behind it. And whatever strength and power is given to them will only be a temporary bestowal.

As we have said, the visitors need human assistance. They also need human leadership. The Collectives do not have that many individuals functioning in this world, and so they need a hierarchy of human authority to serve them. They need the infrastructures you have already built. This again is why they did not visit at an earlier time. This is why the Intervention has been delayed until this era in human development. The Intervention needs governments; it needs religions; it needs all of this functioning structure through which its organization can flow.

> People in positions of great economic power and wealth, if they are deemed cooperative and receptive, will be reached as well.

Therefore, at the outset they must gain alliances. They must gain followers. They must gain assistance from individuals, especially those whom they deem to be in positions of power and authority. We have already spoken of this in the first set of our briefings. And yet it needs to be repeated, for you must understand that these things are happening and have happened already

There are those individuals in positions of power in commerce and government who are already in liaison with the Intervention. Their numbers will grow, and their strength and influence will grow if the Intervention is not stopped and if public education cannot be successfully generated.

The next group of individuals who have been targeted are leaders of your religious organizations. Those amongst them who are deemed receptive and cooperative will be targeted and ideas and information will flow into their minds until such time as a direct encounter can be arranged. What will be offered to each of them is the promise that their particular religious organization and teaching will become predominant in a new world order. And even beyond that, it will be promised to each of them that their religious teaching, being greater than the others, will be able to extend beyond the world and have influence in the Greater Community itself. What devout religious leader could resist this temptation to have their tradition grow and extend even beyond the confines of this world? Not all leaders will be contacted. Only those who are deemed to be receptive and cooperative and who could become sympathetic and functional within the Intervention itself.

> The Intervention needs governments; it needs religions; it needs all of this functioning structure through which its organization can flow.

> The next group of individuals who have been targeted are leaders of your religious organizations.

Interventions are part of your own human history. We understand that such things have happened countless times. As greater nations attempt to overtake weaker ones, they seek to seduce the leaders of those weaker groups and nations with promises of power and authority and gifts of technology, mere trinkets. How effective this has been. Yet this is not unique to your world. It happens throughout the Universe.

Leaders of your religious organizations will be given the promise of pre-eminence in your world. Even their beliefs will be acknowledged, yet this is but deception again. The visitors do not care about your religions. They believe they are only the folly and the superstitions of humanity. Having no religion of their own that you could possibly recognize and understand, they will seek to use yours in order to garner your allegiance to them. The Collectives believe this is entirely ethical, for they believe that humanity will destroy the world without their Intervention. This is of course untrue, but this is their belief. And they feel that such methods are needed to secure the end that they are attempting to achieve. The Collectives justify these behaviors because they believe in the superiority of their race and in the necessity of their mission here in the world.

> The visitors do not care about your religions. They believe they are only the folly and the superstitions of humanity.

Their thought is, "Why let the natives ruin the world when we can run it for them and we can teach them the great value and benefit of our collective community?" This is why you must not view the Intervention in a superstitious manner. The visitors are not angels, and they are not demons. They are driven by the same needs that drive humanity, and they will employ many of the same techniques that humanity has attempted to employ, though on a far lesser scale, in order to achieve their goals.

Next, the inducement will be focused upon two distinct groups of individuals. Actually, these are not groups of individuals, but really classifications, of individuals. The first are those who are considered psychic and sensitive. The inducement here is to validate their sensitivity and to induce them into the collective mind of the

Intervention itself. Here these individuals will be encouraged to support the Intervention, and their own beliefs regarding the frailties and the sinfulness of humanity will be encouraged. And their hope that some greater power from beyond the world will come to rescue humanity from its own demise will be greatly encouraged. Here it will be taught to them that they are part of a greater association of life that is demonstrated by the Intervention itself. Here their religious views and aspirations will be encouraged but directed towards the Collectives.

These individuals will be told to trust in the extraterrestrial presence that is in the world, that it is here to uplift humanity, to transform humanity, and to rescue humanity from its own errors. They will be encouraged to become its representatives, to become its speakers, to inspire others to give their faith and their trust to the extraterrestrial presence and to become part of this movement in consciousness, this great evolutionary change that is occurring in their midst. Yet these individuals, without knowing the real nature or intentions of the Intervention, will unwittingly become its speakers and its representatives. Having become part of the visitors' Pacification Program, these people will now pacify others and bring them to the Intervention.

The visitors are not angels, and they are not demons. They are driven by the same needs that drive humanity.

So while the visitors seek liaison with individuals in positions of power in government and religion, they also seek to establish emissaries throughout the human population. For those sensitive individuals who cannot become receptive to and cooperative with the Intervention, their skills and abilities will be thwarted and offset. If such individuals begin to gain an insight into the real nature of the

Intervention, they can become the target of real mental disruption. In addition, amongst the sensitives and the psychics, there will be a search for those few individuals living in the world today who have an inborn and intuitive awareness of the depositories. The search for these individuals is underway.

The visitors understand that the key to human allegiance is the quest for power, wealth and spiritual fulfillment. Here people will operate against their own best interests if they believe that their activities are ordained and supported by a greater power. We have spoken of this already in our first series of discourses.

They also seek to establish emissaries throughout the human population.

Yet again we must elaborate on this point. Perhaps you will see those who claim to be psychic and sensitive being supportive and encouraging people to trust and to believe in the presence of the visitors, believing that the visitors represent a spiritual awareness, a spiritual force, even evolution itself. The visitors will tell them, "Look, we have no war. We live in peace and cooperation. You have not achieved these things. Therefore, trust that we are able to give them to you and teach you the ways of cooperation and teach you how to live in peace, harmony and equanimity."

The visitors understand that the key to human allegiance is the quest for power, wealth and spiritual fulfillment.

Who amongst the idealistic can resist such a temptation, having lost faith in the human spirit? Having disavowed human institutions to a certain extent, they now look to the heavens for help, for inspiration and for salvation itself. And when they are taken by the visitors or contacted by the visitors, such predispositions put them in the perfect position to become receptive to the Intervention and to become emissaries for the Intervention.

Those who will not cooperate will be given confusing informa-tion. They can even be tormented mentally unless they call upon the power of the Unseen Ones, the Angelic Presence, to help them. And they must gain a strong position of resistance to the Intervention with a real understanding of its motives. Our words will give them strength and encouragement. This in part is why our message is so urgently needed in the world today.

The next group who will be contacted will be those who are zealous representatives of their own reli-gious traditions. Their fundamentalism is very close in many respects to the philosophy and the mentality of the Collectives. The Collectives support only one view of reality and only one view of community, and they hold this in reverence almost to the point of it being a religious emphasis. Those people who are zealous, especially those who are filled with anger and resentment against the world and against those who they see oppose them, will become prime candidates to espouse a cooperation with the Collectives and the destruction of those who stand against the Collectives.

The next group who will be contacted will be those who are zealous representatives of their own religious traditions.

This is a very difficult and dangerous situation, for the visitors will use human allegiance and their human emissaries to carry out their destructive activities in the world. It will not be the visitors who will destroy those who will not and cannot cooperate. It will be the visitors' human counterparts, their human representatives, who will carry out such destruction. In this way, the real nature and purpose of the Intervention remains hidden and such acts of violence will simply be attributed to human error and to human violence and demonstrate the need for the Intervention. For the visitors again will say, "Look at these terrible acts of violence! We are not violent. We do not come with weapons of war. We do not destroy you. This is the result of human ignorance and human depravity. We will teach you how to outgrow all of these things." So even the violence that is perpetrated by the Intervention will be used by the visitors to support their superiority and to contribute to the illusion that they themselves do not use deception, manipulation or force to gain their advantage.

Clearly, there are individuals in your world who are very zealous in representing their religious beliefs and aspirations. The Unseen Ones have told us much about this, and we of course have seen this in many other worlds. It is not unique to humankind. Yet it is a form of blind passion, and blind passion fueled by anger and hostility becomes a consuming force for the individual, a force which can be highly manipulated and is vulnerable to usurpation by the Intervention itself.

Such zealous people will rally a movement of strict adherence and will draw out those who oppose such a strict adherence. Violence will be wrought upon the unbelievers, and they shall be cast aside. In this way, through the eyes of the Intervention, those who oppose the Intervention and those who cannot willingly support it will be identified and will be sorted out amongst the many people who dwell in your world. And the sifting will happen at the level of human interaction. In this way, the visitors will recognize their true adversaries and their potential adversaries. And having gained now a network of human representatives who are zealous in supporting and advancing their religious causes, the Intervention will use these individuals as the medium through which violence will be perpetrated. All the while, the visitors will remain seemingly above and beyond such activity and behavior.

You may stop at this point and wonder, "Well, how can such things occur? This seems so extreme! This seems so negative, so awful!" But for anyone who has studied human history, you will see demonstrations of all of these things we are speaking of—religious manipulation, interbreeding, violence wrought upon adversaries, particularly in situations where native populations are encouraged to accept and to receive their new visitors. It is far easier to govern one who believes in your cause and is cooperative than it is one who is simply being subjugated. Humanity has great strength to throw off the shackles of subjugation. And so the Intervention will seek to use these inducements to gain as much cooperation and as much belief in their presence and in their cause as is possible. They will employ individuals in positions of power, those who have great sensitivities and psychic abilities and those who are zealous representatives of their religious traditions, to foster and generate such cooperation.

For the vast majority of people in your world, the Intervention will be unknown and completely hidden. Yet for those who become aware of it, either because they have been taken, or because they have witnessed evidence of the Intervention in your world, these individuals will either be encouraged to believe and to support the Intervention or they will be cast aside and tormented by it. Already, there are individuals in your world, we understand, who have been cast aside and who are tormented, who have seen and felt and recognized things that they cannot incorpo-

> For the vast majority of people in your world, the Intervention will be unknown and completely hidden.

rate into their understanding. Finding no compassion amongst their human fellows, they deteriorate into depression and into self-disassociation.

Here the visitors attempt to either bond you to them or try to switch you off. Only one who is strong with Knowledge will be able to resist the inducement and to find insulation and freedom from torment. That is why learning The Way of Knowledge must be encouraged.

Here you must learn to counteract your own tendencies to want to see a good outcome and take a hopeful position, which makes you vulnerable to persuasion and manipulation. You must see with clear eyes, sober eyes, without hope and fear, but with a clarity of Knowledge within you. If you can gain this awareness, all that we are telling you and all that we are reminding you of will become so evident to you. You do not need to be living in space to see these things. You do not need to have traveled around the Greater Community to understand what is occurring in your world. But you do need assistance. You do need a larger perspective. You do need a greater understanding. You need the encouragement to see clearly and not to give over your mind, your heart or your world to any force that promises you peace, power, freedom or equanimity. For these things must be born of your own nature and your own activities. They cannot be forced upon you or even given to you. You must achieve them and build them yourselves.

At this point, at the outset, you must become informed. And you must become sober and wise. You may doubt our words, yet you will not find such a reassurance anywhere else, for we are the only representatives of your allies. The other extraterrestrial forces who are actually involved in your world, though they may try to

THE THIRD BRIEFING: THE INFLUENCE UPON HUMANITY

present themselves as the allies and the saviors of humanity, are only here to gain your allegiance and to take control of your world. You have no friends amongst them. The situation is very clear but very difficult, very challenging. It is not ambiguous. Though you have many questions about life in the Greater Community and the reality of the Intervention itself, many questions that even we cannot answer successfully, you can still see clearly what is happening and mount the necessary effort to resist it. You have the individual and collective power to do this.

Though the visitors have a superior technology, the success of their entire mission rests upon their ability to persuade and to encourage human allegiance. You have the power to resist this. You have the power to see through the deception. It is not technology that you need now but awareness, discernment and inner conviction. The situation is very clear, if you can see it, and once you see it, you will have no doubt as to what is occurring, and you will look about and you will see with great concern how others are mindlessly going along, or even encouraging the very thing that will take from humanity its own freedom and self-determination.

Though the visitors have a superior technology, the success of their entire mission rests upon their ability to persuade and to encourage human allegiance.

As we have said, this whole phenomenon is not some mystical or complex situation that is beyond human understanding. It is nature being acted out subtly, with great skill. It is a greater power trying to take advantage of a weaker one. Such an activity will either succeed or fail, depending upon the strength and the determination of the weaker force. The Collectives are prevented from simply taking over your world. Their competitors will not allow it, and the ruling organizations that govern commerce and trade in this region in which your world resides, will not permit it. A Collective will function according to the rules, but beyond those rules it will use any means it can to secure its goals and to fulfill its mission.

Great inducement is being placed upon the world. It has many avenues of expression and emphasis. Yet it is all aimed at one goal—to move humanity to a position of trust, allegiance and subservience to the Intervention itself. This completely conceals the real nature of the occupation that is being attempted in your world. This occupation will become easily recognized once it is fully established, yet by then it will be too late for you to offset its influences without great struggle and sacrifice.

Therefore, we urge you and strongly encourage you to place this phenomenon at the forefront of your awareness and attention. You have time to stop the Intervention. It can be stopped. You have the power and the collective strength to do this. It is not technology that is your disadvantage. It is ignorance. It is greed. It is hostility. It is naivete. These are the things that will undermine humanity's strength. It is these things that will enable the world to be overtaken without war and without violence being carried out on a large scale. But it is the power of Knowledge within you that will make all the difference in preventing this, once you gain the eyes to see and can understand the situation clearly.

The Collectives

Societies exist in the Greater Community at every conceivable level of social and spiritual development. This ranges from pre-agricultural societies all the way up to empires, Collectives, and other kinds of organizations established between worlds for mutual defense and trade. At every level of this evolution, there are countless expressions. Yet as we have said, there are vast regions of the Galaxy that are unexplored and sparsely populated, where many societies live in secret. And there are many cultures that have never even been discovered.

In our previous discourse, we gave the analogy of the Galaxy being linked together with a series of routes, like a roadmap in your world. There are major avenues of travel, there are secondary avenues of travel, and there are areas where no "roads" exist at all.

The impressions that we would like to give you regarding the Greater Community are most relevant to your position in space and are most descriptive of the environments that are in close proximity to your world. Yet your range of vision is still extremely limited, and you cannot see beyond the closest planets even in your Solar System.

Your attempts at radio communication are futile because no one uses this kind of technology for interplanetary communication.

Travel in the Universe is greatly accelerated by your standards but is still very slow, given the enormity of the physical landscape. Large empires and Collectives can only extend themselves where they have established an infrastructure nearby. Managing distant outposts is very difficult logistically and has other hazards regarding the intervention of other races, as well as problems with regional jurisdictions and disputes. For this reason, in sparsely populated areas of the Galaxy, the Collectives will not be found. Even large empires may rarely send resource explorers to these regions, for they are far too distant, and even if discoveries could be made, the logistical problems in sending supplies and gaining access to these resources are formidable. To complicate the matter further, in more populated areas in the Galaxy, there are regional rules of conduct. So nations are not that free to move anywhere they want to go in their explorations.

Of course, we cannot expect the human family to understand this. Your current perspective is that the Universe is really there to be explored and to be taken for your own advantage. But, alas, you are not the first ones to arrive there. And there are many civilizations and empires that are far older than anything that humanity has established so far on Earth.

Wars and great conflicts do occur in the Universe, but they are relatively rare. Rebellions and internal disputes are more common, but wars between large nations and empires in the Universe are far more rare than you might think. We cannot speak for other Galaxies, for we have never ventured there. But from what we know of this Galaxy and of our own travels, we know these things to be quite true.

Humanity is still discovering many secrets about technology, and so this is where it places its hope and its promise. However, amongst more advanced nations, power of influence in the Mental Environment is the far greater arena of influence. For as we have said, technology can be purchased and copied. That is not where the real advantages will usually be found.

However, resources are valuable, and therefore, the destruction of natural environments is generally looked on with disfavor. To preserve these resources and environments, most resource explorers including Collectives will attempt to persuade the native race to come into alliance with them rather than try to overtake that race by force. This strategy is also understood by many advanced civilizations, who have learned through much trial and error and through many difficult periods in the history of their worlds. As societies become more technologically advanced, the need for resources is greater and the preservation of natural resources becomes a greater emphasis. In many cases, home worlds have outstripped their own planets' resources, even to the point where these worlds have become barren and unproductive.

> Collectives will attempt to persuade the native race to come into alliance with them rather than try to overtake that race by force.

This gives evidence as to why your world is viewed with such great interest amongst those few races, relatively speaking, who are aware of you. Biologically rich, rich in resources, strategically important and accessible to many of the Collectives who live in this part of the Galaxy, it is a true prize.

Your proximity to areas that are fairly well inhabited holds both a disadvantage and an advantage for you. The disadvantage, of course, is that your world will be recognized and is within reach of Collectives, which are but one form of social structure in the Universe. The advantage for you, however, is that your world cannot be conquered, for you live in a region that is governed by rules of conduct. If your world existed in a very remote part of the Galaxy, where such rules of conduct were not established, then your world could be taken by force. It could be taken by resource explorers, by pirates, by large nation states, by anyone who could gain access to it and maintain control and authority.

So the fact that you live in a more, shall we say, "civilized" part of the Universe, does give you some degree of protection. In this region, where we also dwell, it is illegal for a new world such as yours to be invaded without the permission of the indigenous race. This means that your world cannot become a part of a larger association unless humanity demonstrates visibly that it agrees to this and that it welcomes intervention.

Your world cannot become a part of a larger association unless humanity demonstrates visibly that it agrees to this and that it welcomes intervention.

Because the Greater Community, especially the area in which you live, is a very competitive environment and because there are many Collectives dwelling here, they tend to hold each other in check and will take legal action against one another if necessary should the basic rules of conduct be violated. Therefore, if one Collective sought to take this world by force, it would be countered by other Collectives who have an interest in this world and by their competitors elsewhere, who would hold these kinds of actions in check.

We cannot expect you to be aware of the details of such a complex situation, but it is important for you to know that the Universe around you is not empty and devoid of life. It is important for you to know that the Universe near your shores is not primitive and unregulated. This will help you understand how the Collectives that are intervening in your world function and how they can be counteracted. This gives you certain advantages, which you must learn to recognize and to employ on your own behalf.

There are other parts of the Universe where great empires exist, and they set their own rules, having few competitors within their regions. And there are many other areas where many nations have joined together in associations, either economic, political or military, or all three, for their mutual trade and defense. These are quite common in areas that are well inhabited in the Universe.

> If one Collective sought to take this world by force, it would be countered by other Collectives who have an interest in this world.

The region in which you live, which encompasses, by your reckoning, a very vast area, contains approximately five thousand stars. We call this a region because that is how it is delineated. This is a very small part of the Galaxy, as you can imagine, but quite large in terms of your interests and needs. In this region, there are important rules of conduct. You have small empires, some of which you would call dictatorships and some of which are more democratic in nature. You have Collectives, which are quite powerful but limited in certain areas of their influence. Yet within this region, all areas that are connected by main thoroughfares of trade are ruled by codes and councils. This is to provide safety and security and to assure that violence does not erupt and grow into all-out warfare. Disputes occur frequently and are handled either through negotiations or through legal procedures.

However, these governing bodies only oversee trade routes, primarily. And they are supported by organizations of states that belong to them for their own mutual benefit and security. Some of these organizations are stronger than others. Yet where you have larger competing powers, the rules of conduct are taken quite seriously and are enforced quite seriously.

In the region in which your world exists, Collectives are not allowed to have armies or military forces. They are allowed to have security forces, however, for their own defense. Being primarily economic institutions, they do seek to protect their interests and their avenues of trade with their own forces. But they do not have large armies such as you might imagine.

> In the region in which your world exists, Collectives are not allowed to have armies or military forces.

They may hire security forces when travelling in areas that are considered unsafe for trade or which are politically unstable between resident nations. But essentially, Collectives, which we would like to take some time to describe now, are not military powers. They are economic powers. Their focus is on trade, resource acquisition and building their alliance amongst worlds such as your own.

There are many Collectives functioning in the region in which your world exists. Some of these Collectives are centered within this region. Some have centers elsewhere and have major satellite establishments here. It is an interesting fact of life that wherever Collectives exist and compete with each other, other nations have established their own defenses against them so that the Collectives cannot intervene in these worlds' trade, commerce and internal affairs. Because we are talking about many nations within a region, many of which have their own military establishments, the Collectives then must abide by certain rules of conduct or face very grave consequences. Being without significant weaponry of their own, they must utilize negotiations, diplomacy and influence as their primary means of accomplishment.

Therefore, those whom you are encountering in the Universe at this time represent highly organized, very hierarchical organizations whose function is resource acquisition and development. Collectives, by and large, are made up of a series of races functioning at different levels of authority and command. Those who really control the Collectives that are functioning in your world have probably not been encountered by anyone in the world yet. You have only recognized the worker classes who are bred to serve in specific functions. Though they are biological entities, their biological codes, their training, their upbringing and their genetic focus have given them very little individuality and individual abilities of reasoning and discernment. They function very much like, well, a collective mind. They are rigidly controlled. They have little or no personal freedom. Their areas of function are very specific and are carried out with impressive efficiency.

Yet Collectives are inherently weak because they are not built on what we call "Knowledge." Therefore, they do not have the strength of insight. They are not creative in their approaches. They tend to mimic one another. They rely upon their structure, their codes of conduct and their ability to manipulate the thoughts and feelings of not only their members but of those races whom they seek to influence. While the Collectives are very powerful in certain respects, they do have inherent weaknesses.

> Collectives, by and large, are made up of a series of races functioning at different levels of authority and command.

Throughout history, Collectives have had great difficulty in maintaining control and authority over their resident populations because they comprise many different racial groups. The worker classes are bred to serve, but even they have certain qualities that the ruling classes of the Collectives find difficult to manage. Revolts have occurred, and Collectives have suffered great losses as a result. They are most certainly imperfect, but more fundamentally, they are not governed by Knowledge, or the power of Spirit. This means that their defenses can be penetrated, their secrets can be uncovered, their activities can be revealed and their deceptions can be comprehended by those who are strong with Knowledge and who are free to see, to know and to act.

> While the Collectives are very powerful in certain respects, they do have inherent weaknesses.

Other nations in regions such as yours deal with the Collectives very, very carefully and do not allow them any kind of penetration into their world's internal affairs. Sometimes the Collectives are viewed as a necessary evil to provide essential resources that are needed by these worlds. The Collectives have great craft and great skill in the areas in which they are strong. And nations which have been able to interact with them successfully have had to maintain a significant distance and be extremely discreet.

> Other nations in regions such as yours deal with the Collectives very, very carefully.

Certainly, interventions such as the one happening in your world would not be allowed by any race that understood its true interests and the realities of life in the Universe. The fact that the Intervention is well underway in your world demonstrates that humanity does not have this awareness and does not have the unity or the social cohesion to resist and to offset unwarranted and unwanted interventions such as this.

We have been told that there are great economic organizations that have interests all around your globe and that employ different nations and different groups in service to these organizations. Perhaps this can serve, then, as an example. But Collectives are far larger. They may encompass hundreds of worlds and planetary establishments and exist across vast reaches of space. They can have significant control and are always interested in gaining new allegiances and new members.

Collectives are but one form of social structure in the Universe. Collectives vary amongst themselves. Some are purely economic and secular in their establishment, focus, theory and philosophy. Others have religious components. However, having religious components does not mean that they are religious in nature. It simply means that part of their philosophy encompasses spirituality, to whatever degree spiritual awareness exists in their members and directs the spiritual awareness or interest, particularly amongst its ruling classes. Yet we have found with very few exceptions that Collectives consider their own survival and their own structure to be the sole focus of their devotion. Their devotion is almost religious in nature, even though their organizations rarely are. If they were strong with Knowledge, they would not be Collectives.

Interventions such as the one happening in your world would not be allowed by any race that understood its true interests and the realities of life in the Universe.

Fundamentally, a Collective is different from an empire in that it has no source home planet. It is a group of planets that are dissimilar which have joined together, usually through conquest and persuasion, and have become a formidable economic force. Whereas an empire is usually centered in one world or in one region by one race, Collectives are made up of many different races. We have never been able to penetrate the hierarchy of a Collective, and so we cannot speak to the composition of its leadership in terms of their racial background. But we know that they are diverse and that they manage their diversity with a strict code of ethics and a hierarchical control that you would find totally oppressive. Certainly, we could not live within such a society although in our cases, we came very close to having to do so.

A Collective is different from an empire in that it has no source home planet.

True democracy, as you would call it, exists in the Universe, even in great manifestations, but it is far more rare than you might think. And certainly any true democracy would have to become very strong in its dealings with the Greater Community, very careful to avoid, if possible, interactions with Collectives and other aggressive kinds of empires.

There is no one empire or Collective in the Universe that is predominant. There is too much diversity and life. There is too much competition. And there have been long-standing disputes between certain nations. Advanced technology is abundant amongst many societies, so the advantages sought are not technological in nature. Though some nations are richer than others, defenses have become formidable in the Universe against violent intrusion. Here again, the Collectives have certain kinds of advantages in that they do not use force. They do not rely upon a military presence to achieve their goals.

There is no one empire or Collective in the Universe that is predominant.

Our native worlds all exist either within the region of your world or nearby. We have all had to deal with Collectives. We have all had to deal with resource explorers from other nations. We have all had to learn to protect and secure our freedom and to become as self-sufficient as possible, in many cases relying upon one another for essential resources for our survival and well-being.

The more self-sufficient a world can become and the more that it can sustain this self-sufficiency, the stronger and the more independent it will be by nature in the Universe. Often nations become dependent upon Collectives because they have exhausted their fundamental resources and must now rely upon trade and commerce for the very basic things they need to live. This, of course, makes them extremely vulnerable to usurpation, and in many cases they become parts of Collectives themselves or extremely dependent upon them.

Often nations become dependent upon Collectives because they have exhausted their fundamental resources.

With the deterioration of your natural environment and the rapid depletion of your essential resources, you are moving into a position of extreme vulnerability and powerlessness in the Universe. This must become part of your understanding. There is little or no awareness of the realities of life, commerce and manipulation in the Universe amongst your people, even amongst your governments and leaders. We have learned a great deal from your transmissions, and we have learned much from the Unseen Ones. Your world, in many respects, has problems common to emerging and developing life throughout the Universe.

With the deterioration of your natural environment and the rapid depletion of your essential resources, you are moving into a position of extreme vulnerability and powerlessness in the Universe.

You have an inherent interest, then, in maintaining and sustaining your world's fundamental resources and in regenerating these resources successfully. Without this, the Collectives will have a great advantage in their inducements. Without this, even if you resisted the Collectives, eventually you would need what they have to offer—raw materials, energy, food production, advanced technology. All these things create a state of dependency, either to a Collective or to many other kinds of states, nations and organizations that are directly involved in trade and commerce. Clearly your world would be at a great disadvantage if you could not bargain successfully for the very things that you need. Eventually, you would have to accept whatever terms are presented to you. The outcome of this then becomes obvious. You are incorporated into other worlds' infrastructure, whether it be a Collective, an empire or an aggressive association of worlds, all of whom are always looking for new territory and new resources.

Your world, in many respects, has problems common to emerging and developing life throughout the Universe.

The Unseen Ones have told us in response to our first set of discourses that many people feel helpless and hopeless in the face of encountering all of these things. We understand this. We have faced such thresholds ourselves, with very grave consequences because we did not prepare in time. However, as we have said, and must continue to emphasize, humanity does have the power and the skill to stop the Intervention and to prevent future interventions of this kind. You have inherent Knowledge that lives within you. This is what we mean by spirituality. You have enough individual power and enough technology to offset the kind of intervention that is occurring in your world at this time. You could drive the Intervention out if you had the will to do it. But you must become educated about the Greater Community, and you must be very clear and sober about what you are dealing with at this time. That is why our counsel is so important, if you can receive it.

Part of the inducement of the Intervention is to discourage those who are aware of its real nature. In other words, for those individuals who become aware of the Intervention, the focus of the visitors then will be to demoralize and to discourage them, to make them feel weak, helpless and impotent in its face, to make them think that they are being visited by enormous powers with unlimited strength, and that they have absolutely no possibility of resisting the visitors' persuasion or offsetting the visitors' presence in the world.

This is but part of the manipulation that is being perpetrated. For those who seem cooperative and receptive, the glorious benefits of collaborating with the visitors will be emphasized. For those who are doubtful about these things or who cannot be persuaded, then discouragement and demoralization will be the primary influence.

Here, then, it is necessary for you to understand that your own sense of weakness and helplessness is not merely a product of your lack of self-trust but is actually part of the manipulation that is being cast in your mental environment. We understand that the governments of your world encourage their populations to feel weak and dependent upon their government's structure and authority. But we are talking about a greater and more pervasive kind of influence here.

Humanity will succumb either because it is persuaded to do so or because it is discouraged from resisting. These are two forms of manipulation with a common goal. Therefore, you must not lose faith. You must learn about life in the Greater Community.

You have strengths and you have weaknesses. The Collectives have strengths and they have weaknesses. Your position in the Universe has advantages and disadvantages. You also have allies who want to see human freedom protected and who want to see humanity emerge into the Greater Community as a free, united and protected world. We support this everywhere, for this is the true spiritual inclination. In the Universe in which you live, there are formidable forces of opposition against this. However there are powerful forces that keep freedom alive and encourage it and nurture it wherever that can be accomplished.

Therefore, understand that if you feel weak and helpless and overwhelmed, part of this feeling comes from the Intervention itself. Here you must gain great confidence in the inherent goodness of humanity and recognize the real value of your freedom. You have never been challenged like this before. Your freedom has never been challenged as a race, as a people, as a world like this before. Yet everyone in the world can at least value the possibility of freedom and whatever freedom they may have at this moment. It is all at risk now.

You have never been challenged like this before. Your freedom has never been challenged as a race, as a people, as a world like this before.

This is where you find your common unity, and this is where you heal your conflicts and your ancient animosities between one another. Here you settle your scores because now they do not matter. What matters is the preservation of human freedom and your pre-eminence in your own world. What matters now is the preservation of your world's resources for your own future survival and security. What matters now is that you recognize the Intervention and take the necessary steps to thwart it and to stop it. This must happen at every level of your societies—at the level of government, at the level of religion, and at the level of the will of the common people.

If your people simply want little trinkets from the Universe, new technological toys to play with, and you would give away your freedom and your autonomy for this, then certainly our words will not be enough.

There are great spiritual forces in the world we know who support this and who encourage it. Yet their influence and their voices can be overshadowed by the effects of the Intervention and by the ignorance of people themselves. In our worlds, emissaries were sent to advise us of the impending danger that we faced from the infiltration of foreign powers into our worlds. We were being seduced as you are now being seduced to join in mutual benefits of trade and commerce. Those of us who were skeptical and those of us who resisted such a persuasion were alienated from our societies and were dissuaded and discouraged and demoralized to a point where we could not have the governing voice, where we could not represent the will of the people.

If your people simply want little trinkets from the Universe, new technological toys to play with, and you would give away your freedom and your autonomy for this, then certainly our words will not be enough. But the education must start somewhere. And it must reach those people who already have a sensitivity to the Greater Community. It must reach those people who value human freedom and do not take it for granted. It must reach those people who have already been affected by the Intervention, either directly or indirectly. It must begin somewhere. You need to know you have allies in the Greater Community, but you also need to know that it will be human strength and human cooperation that will turn the tide in your favor. We cannot intervene beyond giving you our counsel.

> It will be human strength and human cooperation that will turn the tide in your favor.

You must understand without ambivalence and confusion the real nature and purpose of the Intervention in the world today. At this moment, your true allies are not present in the world. They are not walking the face of your world. They are not dwelling in your world. They are not influencing your governments and people in positions of power. They are not contacting your sensitives and your psy-

> At this moment, your true allies are not present in the world.

chics. They are not trying to persuade those who are religious in their views.

We speak for your true allies. Our counsel is to give you perspective, understanding and sobriety and to help you offset the influences that are being cast upon you and have been cast upon you now for decades. You have the power to resist. You have the power to unite. You have the power to cast off this influence.

> You have the power to resist. You have the power to unite. You have the power to cast off this influence.

The Collectives do not believe you will resist, and so they are less careful than perhaps they should be in influencing you. They think this project will be time-consuming but easy and that the ultimate goal will be achieved without great difficulty. We must then speak to those people who are ready and able to respond. There is no other problem or dilemma in your life as critical as this. Anything that you establish on your own behalf for your nation, for your group, for your culture or your religious tradition will be lost in the face of the Intervention. You do not want to be part of a Collective. You must trust us in this regard and consider our words seriously. There is no freedom there. You will become nothing but servants bonded to your new masters. And though those of you who represent your masters will have certain privileges, you will all be enslaved. And the power then to resist, though it can still be mustered, will have much greater costs and consequences.

> You do not want to be part of a Collective. You must trust us in this regard and consider our words seriously. There is no freedom there.

To those governing powers observing the Collectives who are intervening in your world, it must appear that humanity welcomes the presence of the Collectives. It must appear from the outside that humanity is in favor of this Intervention. That is why there is such a great effort to secure emissaries for the Intervention and to have individuals in positions of power and leadership advocate for the presence of the visitors and affirm the visitors' promises of greater wealth, power, freedom and peace. Can you understand what we are telling you here? This is a deception, both within your world and beyond.

Until there is a strong voice resisting the Intervention that is made known and public, it will appear to outside observers that the Intervention is being welcomed by humanity and is being advocated by humanity. Already, the Intervention has many speakers and representatives, but few vocal critics. Even your vocal criticism creates problems for the Intervention. Even for people to speak out and say, "No, this is wrong! We are being visited against our will! We are being persuaded and manipulated against our will! This must not happen! We do not welcome this! And we demand that the visitors leave!" Until these voices are heard, it will appear to governing bodies and to those who compete with these Collectives, that they are here with human consent. Even to arouse a public outcry would have great benefit here for you.

> Already, the Intervention has many speakers and representatives, but few vocal critics.

It is not that you have to physically remove the visitors. Instead, you have to demonstrate your displeasure with their presence and with their activities. You have to demonstrate sobriety regarding their inducements and their deceptions. And you have to speak out against their attempt to interbreed with humanity, to create a new leadership here. You have to speak out against the abduction of people against their will. For these things are being carried out in secret. Even outside authorities do not know this is happening.

> Raise your voice against the Intervention, and the Intervention is put at risk. Resist the Intervention and the Intervention must stop.

We must keep emphasizing these things so that you can see and understand clearly. Raise your voice against the Intervention, and the Intervention is put at risk. Resist the Intervention and the Intervention must stop and the Collectives must find other ways to gain your attention and your allegiance.

As we said in our previous discourses, no one should be setting foot on your soil without your expressed consent. Your allies would not come here without this expressed consent even though at an earlier time your allies did attempt to reach certain individuals in the world, in the face of the Intervention. Yet generally speaking, no true ally of humanity would intervene in human affairs.

No one should be setting foot on your soil without your expressed consent.

Do not think you can persuade those workers in the Collectives whom you will most likely meet in your face-to-face encounters. They have not the discernment or the will to understand your perspective. They are only carrying out their duties as they have been bred to do. Though they are biological beings and still have the potential for Spirit, the likelihood of you being able to persuade them is very, very limited. They are functioning mindlessly. They do not have the moral foundation you have. Personal freedom is unknown to them, and they do not value it, having been taught that personal freedom is chaotic, unruly and destructive. They would not accept your pleas and your admonitions. And even those who manage and control them, though having greater authority, will not be able to comprehend your complaints or your persuasions.

This is not how the Intervention will be stopped. It will not be stopped by your creating dissension amongst its ranks. The Intervention will be stopped because you have created a voice against it and your people are united in preventing it from happening in the world. At this moment, alien craft come and go at will. People are taken at will. Biological resources are taken at will. Access to individuals in positions of power are made at will. There is not the collective agreement and resistance necessary to offset any of these intrusions, any of these violations of your fundamental rights. This must change. And it must start with someone. It must start with you and with others like you who have a greater awareness and sensitivity. It must start with those who can respond to a message such as ours and who have the inner trust to know that we are speaking the truth.

The Intervention will be stopped because you have created a voice against it and your people are united in preventing it from happening in the world.

What They Want

As we have said, those who are intervening in your world today want to gain control of this world for obvious reasons and for reasons that are not so obvious. They see this world as a great prize, rich in resources, governed by a race that they believe is unruly and unworthy to be the stewards of such a wondrous place. They also value your world, as we have said, because of its strategic importance and because of the hidden depositories that exist in many parts of the world.

But this does not fully answer the question as to what the visitors really want. Here we must open another door into the darker side of the Intervention and, in doing so, reveal more to you the nature of commerce as it exists in this part of the Galaxy.

As we have said, the Intervention is primarily a set of commercial forces, not military forces. They view your world for its prospects, for its resources, for its strategic importance and for its hidden treasures. But what you must understand at this point is that they also value *you*.

As we have emphasized throughout our briefings, they need human assistance to establish themselves in your world. They need the human infrastructure. They need human government and religion. They need your assistance to establish their operations here fully and reliably. And they will provide you a semblance of your former life in order to maintain human order and allegiance to the best of their ability. In order to accomplish and to maintain this, however, they will have to establish a very deep network of deception that we have been describing all along.

Here you must understand that they regard *you* as a resource as well. They do not consider you to be their equals. They do not value your religions, your cultures or your customs. They see you primarily as one of the resources of the world. As such, they seek to take advantage of you in all the ways that they can that they deem to be profitable and valuable to their interests.

To them, you are a potential asset. As an asset, you are valued only in what you are worth to them, how you may assist them and what you may be worth as an entity and as a resource in and of yourself. You must stop to consider what this really means. It means that they consider you to be a biological resource, part of a network of resources that exists within this world. In this, they view you much the same way that you view domesticated animals that you use as a resource. You use these animals for a variety of reasons, we understand. And this is common in the Greater Community in worlds where such animals can be used as a food resource. We understand that you use your animals in many different ways, to provide many different kinds of benefits and substances and so forth. This is how you appear to those who are visiting your world, to the Intervention. They do not consider you their equal. They consider you their resource.

> They consider you to be a biological resource, part of a network of resources that exists within this world.

What you may not understand is that each year thousands of people are taken and not returned to the world. These people are not simply conditioned. They are kept. Some of them perish in captivity. Some of them do not survive the process of their capturing. Some become sick and die. Those that cannot survive and are still seen as useful to the Intervention are used as a biological resource. That means that their blood, their body parts, everything is used according to its value in the Greater Community. In the Greater Community, biological resources such as blood, plasma, DNA, bone marrow, skin and body organs can be used for their chemical substances. From these, medicines are made. From these, new life forms are bred. These substances are valuable commodities in certain parts of the Greater Community.

Each year thousands of people are taken and not returned to the world.

If those who are captured and not returned survive, they will be used for other purposes. Should the Intervention gain complete control of your world, many people who are considered to be undesirable, or who do not fit into the social patterns established through the Intervention, will be used as biological resources in this way.

Perhaps this is shocking, but you can understand this, for this is how you treat your animals as biological resources—to be used for food, for clothing, for medicines, for fuel. In the Greater Community, biological resources are very valuable because they can be used and altered for a variety of purposes as we have mentioned—for medicinal purposes, for life support purposes and for the breeding and generation of new species.

This is why many of your animals are taken. They are not simply taken to provide blood products for the interbreeding program. They are taken because these blood products themselves are highly valuable and can be traded very successfully.

In technological societies such as the Collectives, biological resources are extremely valuable and difficult to find in the Greater Community. As we have said repeatedly, your world is viewed as a biological storehouse. So while the visitors want the mineral resources of your world, they also want things that are much more elemental to the needs of life. They need water. They need oxygen. They need blood. They need the resistance factors in blood. They need plasma. They need the biological elements that constitute life and that are fundamental to life everywhere.

This means that they need *you* as a biological resource. It is one thing to consider that your world will be used to serve other powers. But the idea that *you* will be used to serve other powers is another matter altogether and represents a further violation of your fundamental rights.

Those that they persuade to become their adherents and their representatives will never be told these things.

This, of course, is entirely hidden from their public agenda. Those that they persuade to become their adherents and their representatives will never be told these things. Part of their Pacification Program is to assure you that they are here for your good and for your redemption and for the preservation of the world. But as we have so often said, it is the preservation of the world for *their* needs. The plants, the animals, the breathable atmosphere and the water are all resources to be used and are valuable in and of themselves, as well as the mineral wealth that exists in this world. But the missing part in all this is *your* role as a biological resource. This is how the Intervention views you—as a resource. This, of course, would never be revealed to those who are being pacified or to those who even today may stand as representatives and apologists for the Intervention. But this is so very true.

You may wonder, where have all the people gone who have disappeared and not returned? You may ask this. Did they all run away? Some indeed were the victims of human violence. Some indeed have run away. But we are talking about many people worldwide who have disappeared, without a trace, without a clue. We know this from studying the transmissions of your governments. We know this from what the Unseen Ones have told us. And we know this because this is evident in the Collectives' intrusions in other worlds. Somehow, mysteriously, individuals begin to disappear at the early stages of these Interventions. And people who recognize that these disappearances are happening will think it is due to the normal but unfortunate circumstances within their own cultures. It will be explained in these terms.

Here you must think of your well-being and the well-being of your family, your children, your friends and your acquaintances, most assuredly. And beyond this, you must consider the well-being of your whole world and the security of human life. As a resource, you will be used, and when your usefulness is over, you will be discarded. This is how resources are used. Some are preserved. Some are used up. Just the way that you use resources in your daily life.

What you think of as the human soul, the spirit of humanity, is not valued by the Intervention. This violation is so complete and so thorough, and it is occurring already in all of its manifestations. Look into this matter and think for yourself. And you shall see for yourself. We are giving you the perspective of looking from the outside in. This gives you an objective view of the circumstances of your world and the forces that are acting upon it.

As we mentioned in our first set of discourses, should the Intervention take full hold and an occupation be established here completely, then the human population will be reduced into an efficient working class. How will this be accomplished without producing outrage and revolution among the human population? It will be accomplished through the disappearance of people. It will be accomplished by the isolation of those who are considered to be uncooperative or dissenting. They will be taken away, to be seen no more. And while there will be the appearance of normalcy in human affairs, behind the scenes everything will be changed and will be managed by a different set of powers.

> While there will be the appearance of normalcy in human affairs, behind the scenes everything will be changed and will be managed by a different set of powers.

It is hoped by the Collectives that this can be accomplished for as long as possible and that a revolution will not begin, for that would be very costly to their endeavors. And very costly to humanity as well. The visitors are here to do business. You are part of the business. Your hands. Your eyes. Your reproductive organs. Your blood. Your plasma. Your biochemistry. This is all part of their business. To them, you are like intelligent livestock—useful, interesting and commercially important.

At the outset, they will treat you with deference, those of you who may encounter them face to face, but they will give you no power. They will not give you a choice. They will only try to convince you of the wisdom of their ways and the necessity of their presence in the world. And should you decline or should you resist, they will make life difficult for you, or they will discard you for later use.

Some of those, we understand, who have not returned to the world were those who fought against them and were eliminated as a result. How do we know these things? We know them because we understand the Collectives. We understand their legal commerce, and we understand their illegal commerce. They want to use every part of the world. And they want to use every part of you. Just like you would want to use every part of the cow or the sheep or any other domesticated animal that you breed for your own purposes.

How do we know that they are doing these things in the world? We know because we are monitoring their communications. Otherwise, we could not fully observe their activities and understand the nature of their involvement here. It is remarkably similar to their involvement in other emerging worlds. What we cannot see, the Unseen Ones have revealed to us.

At the outset, they will treat you with deference, those of you who may encounter them face to face, but they will give you no power.

We know from their transmissions, their communications with their bases within the world and their satellites beyond the world, that many of their "specimens," as they refer to you, have either perished or had to be used for other reasons. However, we know from their earth transmissions that many people are disappearing. So it is not difficult for us to see the connection.

In their attempt to breed a new leadership for humanity, a hybridized person, they need all of these biological resources that we are describing.

What we are speaking of here is the most hidden and secret part of their agenda, the part that they will never reveal to you willingly, the part that you may never see without great assistance. This is the most secret of their activities. They sell biological products on what you would call a "black market" in the Universe. But the value of these products and the demand for them is indeed significant.

In most places where commerce has been established, such as in your vicinity, such trade is illegal, for it is considered to be morally and ethically reprehensible. But with so many technological societies existing in the Universe and biological resources such as exist in your world being as rare as they are, the demand for these fundamental elements is considerable.

Many technologically advancing nations have outstripped their own world's biological resources to the extent that they must find them elsewhere, and they must trade and barter for them as one of their primary endeavors. This is not simply food products, minerals and metals and elements such as this. It is also the need for biological products such as we have described, which are abundant in your world and which are abundant within the human family.

In their attempt to breed a new leadership for humanity, a hybridized person, they need all of these biological resources that we are describing.

What we are speaking of here is the most hidden and secret part of their agenda.

So when someone asks, "What do they want?" the appropriate answer is, "They want your world and its resources. And they want *you* and *your* resources." As we have said, this is the most hidden of their agendas. But it is necessary for you to know because this makes the violation complete.

The visitors do not "hate" humanity. They are not cruel and murderous in the sense that you might think. They just view you as a resource the way you view your animals as a resource. To them, though you have intelligence, they consider that you are irredeemably chaotic and unruly, and they do not understand your deeper motivations. They see your technology as being in a rather adolescent phase, and they look at your destructive behaviors with concern, anxiety and repulsion. Being without Knowledge, the spiritual foundation, they do not see that what they are perpetrating upon your world is ethically or morally reprehensible. It is merely an opportunity to fulfill their practical necessities

As we have said, they seek to bring humanity into their Collective, but this is only a very select part of your population. And here you would not be at the upper levels of their hierarchy. For all the other people in the world, what will happen to them if the Intervention is complete, if the occupation can be established completely?

So when someone asks, "What do they want?" the appropriate answer is, "They want your world and its resources. And they want you and *your* resources."

We have been reluctant to tell you certain things because we do not want to lose your attention. We do not want you to turn away in denial, thinking that you cannot face these matters. So we have tried to be extremely careful in the way that we have presented the situation. But in spite of this, there are certain things you must know and that you cannot readily see from your vantage point. We had to learn about these realities ourselves though we had assistance such as we are providing for you. But the reprehensible nature of the Collectives and their lack of morality and ethics is something we have had to face. That is why we avoid the Collectives in our own worlds, where they cannot penetrate.

There are many nations in the Universe that have created alliances to protect themselves from Collectives such as these, particularly in well-inhabited areas of the Galaxy. This is why many of the Collectives' activities are governed by trade unions and regional governing powers and authorities. They are held in check by many other forces who do not want to fall under their persuasion or their control. Even many of their trading partners look at them with anxiety. And even if they are forced to engage in commerce with Collectives, they must protect themselves from the Collectives' influence.

Resources are precious in the Universe—mineral resources, water resources, biological resources, food resources. Large technological societies such as the Collectives have an enormous need for resources for their own maintenance. Their commerce is based upon the acquisition of all these things and on the exploration for new sources. This, of course, makes them primarily interested in emerging worlds such as your own, which are emerging within regions where they have influence and power.

There are many nations in the Universe that have created alliances to protect themselves from Collectives such as these.

Consider our words. Now we will tell you what you must do.

A Call to Action

I t has been our mission to observe the alien Intervention in the world today and to provide to you our commentaries and our perspective. It is a difficult task and a difficult message. We understand the problems that people may have in receiving this communication. They may question our method of communicating. They may question, certainly, our reality and identity and the trustworthiness of our words. They may question the reality that we are presenting. And perhaps the temptation to deny these things will be great for some people.

Yet what will really enable you to hear our words and to know their authenticity will be your ability to respond with the deeper knowing within yourself. Throughout our discourses, we have referred to the reality of Knowledge, the Spiritual Intelligence that lives within you. We have spoken of its central importance in your preparation for the Greater Community. We have spoken of it as the true power that enables you to see beyond all the deceptions and manipulations of the Intervention. We have spoken of it as the inherent power that the Collectives do not use and do not recognize—Knowledge. This Knowledge is not like a military power. It is not something that you can use to gain things by force or to overwhelm or dominate others. It is the greater Spiritual Intelligence that you share with the Creator.

Humanity has a great challenge before it and is facing a great risk in its emergence into the Greater Community. Therefore, it is necessary to find the strength that will enable you to unite your peoples and to take your place in the Greater Community as a free and self-determined race. This power must come from within people and must be reinforced by the greater forces for good that exist both within your world and in the Greater Community.

There will perhaps be people who will reject our words and counsel and reject what we are presenting altogether. They may have their own preferences in the matter. They may have their own fear and sense of inadequacy. Perhaps they have fallen prey already to the persuasions of the Intervention and do not wish to consider that they may be in error. Perhaps they are just too afraid to face this great challenge. Perhaps they want to escape into their personal concerns and preoccupations. But what is really being called for here is the power and the presence of this Spiritual Intelligence we call Knowledge, which is the source of your real conscience. Yet what you may not realize is that this is the very source and bond of all spirituality in the Universe. The expressions of spirituality and the rituals of spirituality, the great Teachers and emissaries of spirituality are too numerous to count in the Universe. The philosophies and the methodologies are unique to cultures and their histories. But at the center is this mysterious and profound power that enables you to see, to know and to act in harmony with the Creator of all life.

Surely our presence and our words can be rejected and denied. But with Knowledge, this will not be the case. For we are certain that we are presenting the truth to the best of our ability. Your allies abroad have sent us here on a mission in great service to humanity. The integrity of our mission and of our presentation is real and genuine. It is not merely a matter of perspective or perception..

We must rely upon this Spiritual Power within you, the reader and the receiver of our message. For indeed, we are revealing more than our words can convey. We are revealing an entire reality of life in the Universe. We are opening the door to the great mysteries that humanity has not yet penetrated, and in some cases has not even considered.

> We are revealing more than our words can convey. are revealing an entire reality of life in the Universe. We are opening the door to the great mysteries that humanity has not yet penetrated,

Though we are very different from you and though we practice our spirituality in ways that are unique to us and that you could not really accommodate, what we emphasize is absolutely fundamental to your being, to your nature and to your reality. Knowledge is not simply a great potential that lives within you. It is the most vital element that can secure your freedom and maintain it, both now and in the future. There is the freedom to live according to your conscience, and then there is the freedom to find Knowledge within yourself. Unless you have the first freedom, it will be much more difficult to find the second. First you must survive and remain free, and then the opportunity is there for you to gain access to the greater Spiritual Intelligence that lives within you. Finding this freedom and this Knowledge gives you insight into the reality and the meaning of life in the Universe. This gives you great promise, and we must emphasize that which gives you this great promise— Knowledge, freedom, strength. These are the things that you must now cultivate.

In the future, the differences between you as human beings will become increasingly less significant. Two things will overshadow them. The first will be forces from the Greater Community, which will challenge your essential right to be in the world as a free race. This puts everyone in the same boat. The second will be the reality of Knowledge within you, which will seek to unite you with others in order to give you this Knowledge, this freedom and this strength. Discovering this Knowledge is not merely an option and not merely the goal of exceptional individuals. It represents the essence of your struggle for freedom.

We place our faith in the essential goodness and potential wisdom that reside within the human family.

Knowledge will reveal this to you and will confirm our words. Beyond your preferences and beliefs, this is most certainly true. We have confidence here, for this is where we place our faith— in the essential goodness and potential wisdom that reside within the human family. Otherwise, our great attempt to sound an alarm and to bring a Greater Community awareness into the world will fail. It will not take effect here. This failure has grave consequences, for humanity does not yet understand its predicament, nor does it understand what it must rely upon in order to achieve success. The Creator wills that humanity be a free race in the Universe, but it is up to you. It depends on what you choose to believe in, what you choose to do and what you choose to emphasize.

The Intervention is very secretive and very clandestine. Only those who have been directly impacted by it or who have been contacted directly are aware of its presence, and they are subject to considerable persuasion and manipulation, as we have described. Therefore, who is in a position to really know on their own accord?

We provide a perspective that you could not have otherwise. We provide insight into important realities about life in the Greater Community that you do not have access to. And we bear witness to those of you who have begun to feel these things already within yourselves. Our message serves as a confirmation of these deeper insights. But the question remains, can you know what you know, can you follow what you know and can you respond from this deeper part of yourself and share this with other people?

Soon we will have to leave the vicinity of your world, for as the first set of discourses was revealed, the Intervention became aware of our presence here and began a thorough and determined search for us. We must escape before this happens, and even here our escape carries with it great dangers for us. Our departure will not go unnoticed. And there will be an attempt to follow us and to find us wherever we go. We cannot return to our home worlds for that would lead to their discovery. We must seek hiding at a greater distance. From that position, we will not be able to witness the ongoing activities of the Intervention.

Therefore, in these two sets of Briefings, we must provide you everything that you will need to proceed on your own. Yet our assistance as observers is soon to come to an end. Even as we present these words, we are prepared to leave. Therefore, we communicate in great haste with a sense of urgency. Yet we must wonder, who can really hear us and take to heart what we are saying? And who will act upon these words with their own inner conviction? We are not here to lead you or to be leaders for humanity. Humanity must have its own leaders. Yet who will assume this mantle of responsibility? Who will have the inner conviction? Who is strong enough with Knowledge to see, to know and to feel the reality of what we are presenting to the point where they can take action and begin to speak out against the Intervention?

We cannot answer these questions. Only you can answer them. We can provide you glimpses into life in the Universe and an essential understanding of the nature and activities of the Intervention and of those who are intervening here. Yet we cannot answer every question and indeed it is not answers that you need as much as the inner conviction to see, to know and to act. Our greatest desire is that we may stimulate this within enough people that a movement will arise to offset the Intervention and to demonstrate humanity's displeasure with its uninvited guests. This would be a beneficial beginning. But it is only the beginning, for there must be an awareness of the reality of the Greater Community. And there must be a sober and profound understanding of what humanity must do in order to secure its freedom and its well-being in this larger and far more complex arena of intelligent life..

> We are not here to lead you or to be leaders for humanity. Humanity must have its own leaders.

It has been our desire not to cast a dark or fearful specter of life in the Universe, for indeed there are many marvelous and wondrous creations, and there are many societies that have achieved very high states of awareness. Yet these still remain in the minority of the manifestations of intelligent life throughout this Galaxy to the extent that we are aware of, and we have met many others who have seen things that we have never seen.

> No one in the world is prepared to give you this counsel, for how could anyone know?

In order for humanity to enter into this new panorama of life, you must have an orientation as to what exists there and what to expect and how you must function and conduct yourselves. No one in the world is prepared to give you this counsel, for how could anyone know? It takes your allies, the Allies of Humanity, to provide this perspective and this orientation. Otherwise, you would feel alone and so vulnerable that you could lose heart and capitulate to the persuasion of those who seek to gain control of you and your world.

We would like now to say something about the individual who is receiving this communication. Marshall Vian Summers is not simply a man who was unwittingly chosen for a great task. He has been sent into the world for this purpose. He is a man who has been sent with a Divine mission, to help prepare humanity for its encounters with the Greater Community and to represent The Greater Community Teaching in the world, a teaching in The Greater Community Way of Knowledge.

Many years ago, there was an attempt on our part to reach him directly. He was called to a location in a mountainous area and was prepared for his contact with us. Several members of our party made the dangerous journey into this world, but unfortunately their mission was never completed. Once they were discovered by the Intervention, they had to destroy themselves and their craft, leaving no evidence behind of our presence in the world. This marked a great failure. And the loss of four very precious individuals. There are only five of us left now. And we again are facing great danger.

The preparation for our contact with this individual has been long and with many delays. First, he had to become the receiver for The Greater Community Teaching. He had to become its first student. Then he had to take a position from which he could represent this new threshold of understanding for humanity. Certain people were called to assist him, not all of whom were able to do so. Many of these delays, which were largely beyond his control, have delayed our presentation. This is why we are late in giving you our discourses and our briefings.

It has been a very great challenge for this individual to receive and to accept such a responsibility. He did not ask for it. Yet he is born with it. And with all the delays, the chance for success has become more of a concern to us. That is why at this time we must speak with great emphasis. And we must repeat our essential message so that we can be sure that it is being heard and understood.

> Every month and every year now is precious. Every month and every year that humanity remains unprepared for the Greater Community, the situation becomes more difficult and more grave.

Every month and every year now is precious. Every month and every year that humanity remains unprepared for the Greater Community, the situation becomes more difficult and more grave. We have had to move twice in our position here in your Solar System. We cannot tell you more, for we do not wish to give evidence of our presence to your adversaries.

In our own histories, for those of us who remain, it was equally difficult to present a very similar message to our own cultures. We were met with disbelief, ridicule, shock. The idea that our worlds could be intervened by forces who were not friendly to us was something that our races were totally unprepared for. We believed, as do you, living in a state of isolation, that we were privileged and had the graces of the Divine powers. We could only assume that the initial visitations, which were carried out as secretly as they are in your world, were for a greater benefit. That was our assumption. It was only when a group such as ourselves met and counseled certain individuals in our respective worlds in order to deliver a warning and an awareness that a real preparation could begin.

Yet we must remain emphatic in our assurance that there is still time for humanity to offset and stop the Intervention. However, for this to happen, this individual must be recognized and assisted. You must speak out yourself on behalf of this message that we are giving, and you must assist him in speaking on behalf of it. He has very little support in the world. There are great obstacles. The Intervention is aware of him and even at this moment is seeking to thwart him.

This message that we are conveying to you has been entrusted to this individual to deliver to you in a pure form, as pure a form as can be achieved. We have confidence that he has been able to do this. He has also been given The Greater Community Teaching, which is the only preparation in the world to prepare people in a Greater Community Way of Knowledge.

We are very honored to be able to present this information. And we regret the many delays that have prevented us from giving it at an earlier time. We are working against powerful forces, and we must await the readiness of those who can receive us and who can plant the seeds that we are presenting here in these Briefings.

We have imparted that which we feel is essential for your well-being and your survival. We have left out many other things that you would perhaps find very fascinating, but which are not central to your need. We have been very concerned not to cloud the essential issue with non-essential details. And indeed too many details simply make our communication seem more inexplicable.

We speak on behalf of your allies, who are substantial and represent many races. All nine of us have come from different worlds, and yet we share the same

> We want for humanity what we want for ourselves, which is self-sufficiency, creativity, freedom from intrusion and life without conflict and war.

mission because we are strong with Knowledge. We want for humanity what we want for ourselves, which is self-sufficiency, creativity, freedom from intrusion and life without conflict and war. The right to be in life in order to achieve a higher purpose and respond to a higher calling that the Creator has provided to all as a potential—this is what we seek to affirm for ourselves and for the human family. Yet as is true in your world, there are powerful forces and persuasions that stand in the way of this discovery and achievement. And so we work behind the scenes to advocate for freedom and Knowledge in all sentient beings, even in the Collectives, even in empires that are aggressive and destructive, even in individuals who are unscrupulous and devious.

Humanity is but at the beginning of its greater accomplishments.

We are aware of many races in the Universe who demonstrate Knowledge and the lack of Knowledge. You will have the opportunity to learn about these things in the future if you can secure your freedom now. Humanity is but at the beginning of its greater accomplishments. Yet its current recklessness, its tribal conflicts and its environmental degradation all threaten the possibility that you will have the chance to achieve a greater state of life for your people.

That which seems to overshadow humanity is the one thing that can unite humanity and bring an end to tribal conflict.

The Intervention seems now as a rude intrusion into an already difficult situation. But as so often is the case, the great demonstrations of nature prove to be redemptive if they can be recognized and utilized accordingly and appropriately. That which seems to overshadow humanity is the one thing that can unite humanity and bring an end to tribal conflict. Every person in the world must learn about the Greater

Community and the truth about the Intervention in the world. They must learn about the Intervention before it fulfills its occupation. Any advancement in this regard is a blessing. Any failure in this regard hurts all life in your world.

Though one individual has been given the burden and the privilege of bringing our message into the world and to receive The Greater Community Teaching, it will be up to many, many people in many cultures to share this understanding and this preparation and to translate it into many different languages in your world. The need for freedom and the desire for freedom are universal. Essentially our message and The Way of Knowledge are about freedom—the freedom to live freely in your own world without bondage to another race and without intrusion or intervention from another race, and the freedom to find Knowledge and to fulfill yourself in your great journey here in physical life. It is all about freedom.

When the religious leaders of the world and the political leaders of the world recognize that they have a fundamental common interest and common mission to defend the human family, then they can bring all of their assets to bear in this regard. This will largely overshadow their disagreements and their hostilities towards one another.

The question then for you is, are you free to know these things that we are speaking of? Are you free to respond? Are you free to speak out against the Intervention? The teaching in freedom starts right now. This is the first step.

It is all about freedom.

This is not a time for ambivalence or complacency. This is not a time to simply project one's grievances and distrust upon the world. To the extent that humanity is divided and unaware of life beyond its borders, it is vulnerable and without real security. Your opposition to one another is misplaced. The truth is, you have no defense against the outside.

Should you successfully defend your right to be the pre-eminent race in this world and to live with freedom and to cultivate freedom within the human family and within human societies, then you will have the opportunity to meet and to know your allies. That will be a great revelation and homecoming for you. In the meantime, there is great work to be done. And everyone has the possibility to do this great work.

The
Teachers'
Commentaries
on
The Allies of Humanity

◆

WHO ARE THE TEACHERS?

As you have allies within the world and within the Greater Community, so you have allies beyond the visible range of life. The Teachers represent the Angelic Presence who watch over humanity. The Allies of Humanity refer to them as the "Unseen Ones." They are here to become a part of your education in Knowledge. No longer in the physical, they now serve those who are regaining the memory of their Ancient Home and with it the nature and direction of their purpose in life.

◆

GREATER COMMUNITY SPIRITUALITY:
A New Revelation

The Problem of Human Denial

Many people, when reading *The Allies of Humanity Briefings,* will become afraid. They will read it as if they think it is real and genuine, which it is, and they will become frightened and want to withdraw. They will want to deny it in some way.

In a way, *The Allies of Humanity* material reveals your weaknesses. It calls upon your strength. It calls upon your inherent wisdom. It calls upon Knowledge, the Spiritual Mind within you, but it also reveals your weaknesses. It reveals your vulnerability. It reveals your lack of control over your own consciousness. It reveals your undefended borders to space. It reveals your assumptions, your preoccupations, and overall your ignorance of life in the Universe.

Here it is important to ask yourself if humanity will ever encounter intelligent life from beyond its world. And if it does, when that happens, how will humanity respond? How will humanity know if its new visitors are friendly or not? How will humanity be able to discern the visitors' motives and their consciousness? How will humanity be able to discern their organization, their methods and so forth?

If you consider these questions seriously, you will realize that you have very few answers. And without answers, perhaps you will become afraid. You will feel your own vulnerability, and you will feel how unprepared people really are for an encounter such as this.

Because most people still think that they are alone in the Universe, that they have always been alone and will always be alone, well, this important set of questions really does not get considered by very many people. And even those who do consider it often think very romantically about life in the Universe and what it will bring humanity and how much humanity will gain from this encounter. They think how interested the visitors will be in humanity's art and culture, history and temperament.

So even amongst the very few people who really consider these questions and think they are important, there is often a great deal of romantic speculation. People are afraid to be realistic regarding life in the Universe because it reveals their weaknesses. When we speak of weaknesses, we are not talking about your lack of technology. Really, what we are talking about is your lack of awareness, your lack of focus in life, your lack of social cohesion in your nations and cultures. Humanity is divided and contentious within itself. This makes you vulnerable to outside forces. But really your vulnerability goes even beyond this because it has to do with your state of mind. It has to do with your view of yourself and your world. It has to do with your assumptions, your illusions and your preoccupations.

It is as if a great storm were building and had been building for some time, but people paid no attention. And then when the storm hits, well, it hits with such fury. It hits with such an impact. People are completely taken by surprise and are outraged and terrified. And yet the signs were there.

Even human science is beginning now to acknowledge the preponderance of life in the Universe as a theoretical probability. Yet who is concerned with what your first great encounters might mean?

As *The Allies Briefings* are presented, there will be all kinds of denial, criticism and repudiation. Why? Why so much rejection over an encounter that everyone really considers to be

Is the Universe limited by human understanding?

very possible? Yet when it is actually accounted for, you will see a great deal of denial. "Outrageous! Ridiculous! Cannot happen!" You will hear scientists say, "Well, it is not possible for another race to get here given the limitations of travel and speed and so forth." How presumptuous! Do human beings dare to presume what other nations and cultures have been able to develop over a long period of time? Is the Universe limited by human understanding? Is it not possible that other races could have far surpassed human accomplishment in technology?

You may say, "Well, of course!" But when faced with the prospect of a real encounter, people sing a very different tune. Their idealism leaves them. Their romanticism is thrown into doubt. Their glorious anticipation is overshadowed with concern and anxiety.

So when *The Allies of Humanity* message is presented, people begin to feel the real core of their fear, their lack of preparation, the weakness of their position. The Allies present a very realistic view of life in the Universe. They are not here to answer every question that you may have, but instead to give you an awareness of what is really occurring in the world today and also to dispel much of the fanciful speculation that surrounds the prospect of humanity encountering other forms of intelligent life. Even fanciful expectation, hopeful expectation, really has fear at its core because you are uncertain, because you do not know, because you are unprepared, because you realize in a moment of honest recognition how vulnerable you really are, living on the surface of your world, exposed to the Universe and undefended.

It is very important to understand why people are afraid.

Think for a moment if you were another race visiting your world and you wanted to just simply observe human behavior. Just observe it, without interfering. Well, you could look down on everything. It is all there. Human activity, human involvements, human conflict, human relationships, human technology, human communication—it is all available to the discreet observer.

Therefore, it is very important to understand why people are afraid. The fear of the reality of contact is deep-seated. Many people have this very glorified view that they are at the pinnacle of God's creation, that their religions are built upon the pre-eminence of human spirituality and human identity. What will happen when they find out that humanity is one little race evolving within a Greater Community of intelligent life? And that this race is actually very weak, divided and insignificant in the vastness of the Creation!

People's religious views cannot tolerate this kind of realization. Many of these views are already being eroded by the discoveries of science that show that the Universe does not revolve around this world, that this world is just a little planet revolving around an insignificant star in a vast Galaxy amongst many. Where is human pre-eminence then? Who are you in the Universe? Are you really important to anyone or anything?

We are asking these questions to bring you into the core of your anxiety because you must confront this within yourself. The inability or unwillingness to do this is really the source of all human ignorance and presumption regarding humanity's place in the Universe and regarding the reality of the extraterrestrial Intervention that is occurring in the world today.

People say, "Well, there is no Intervention happening here. How ridiculous! It is all the fancy of certain people and their need for attention or their boredom or something." What are you really hearing here but an excuse? This is the way that one pacifies oneself from experiencing real anxiety.

> We are asking these questions to bring you into the core of your anxiety because you must confront this within yourself.

If you could consider this rationally and objectively, you would say, "Well, of course we would be visited at some point! I mean, if there is intelligent life in the Universe, someone out there must know that we exist here." And if you are not limited by the limitations of humanity's science, that opens the door to many more possibilities.

If you can ask these questions, you might think to yourself, "Yes, of course humanity will be encountered. Yes, our resources will be scrutinized. Yes, our world will be evaluated. Yes, there are other powers in the Universe that would perhaps want our world to be part of their organization. And yes, they would want to take advantage of this beautiful place in some practical way."

You see, these observations are so obvious. These speculations, if you could call them that, are so reasonable, but people will not consider them. They will not face them because of their anxiety, because of their fear. In fact, the reality of life in the Universe, the encounter with life in the Universe and the Intervention itself together represent the most denied reality in the world today. People will think, "It is not important. I have my job. I have my family. I have, you know, my own daily problems. I mean, why should it matter to me?" What are you talking about? If there is an Intervention going on in the world, do you think that it is not relevant to you and to your life and to what will happen to you?

> The reality of life in the Universe, the encounter with life in the Universe and the Intervention itself together represent the most denied reality in the world today.

Do you see here? This is "isolationist thinking." *The Allies Briefings* bring home the reality that humanity's isolation is over! But the isolationist thinking continues, unabated. Unless you have a direct encounter with forces from the Greater Community where your life is disturbed or upset in some way, well, you will just continue on thinking the way you have always thought, living upon the assumptions that you have always lived upon, oblivious to the greater realities that are shaping your life and destiny. And how can God reach you to tell you to become alert and aware, to make you responsive to these greater realities that are changing your life and destiny?

People love the idea of a God out there that will throw them a life preserver when they are drowning, but the idea that God will interfere in their life and show them something they really don't want to see, well, that is really a test of faith, isn't it?

That is exactly what is happening today. That is why the teaching in Greater Community Spirituality is in the world because this is God's message to alert humanity to this greater reality and to prepare humanity. The awareness is not enough. If the awareness engenders primary anxiety and fear, people will not know what to do. They will say, "Oh, my God! What do we do?" And they don't know what to do because they have never had to respond to this directly before. That is why God's message brings with it the preparation so people can begin to think like they live in a Greater Community. Then they can begin to become aware that there are Greater Community realities out there that are going to have a direct impact on them, their lives and their world.

The preparation must give you this greater awareness and consciousness, this sensitivity. Otherwise, you are like an ant colony in a field that is about to be plowed under. And the poor ant colony has not a clue of what is about to happen. Up until the moment of their destruction, well, life will be as it has always been.

But you are not ants, and you have a consciousness. You can consider the future, and you can think about things that are beyond your visible range. And you can consider yourself living within a larger arena of life, both within the world and beyond the world within a Greater Community. As you develop this Greater Community awareness, you begin to see that your world is a very special place, with wonderful attributes. And you may think, "Well, of course others would be interested in our planet. And interested in us,

How can God reach you to tell you to become alert and aware, to make you responsive to these greater realities that are changing your life and destiny?

not because we are magnificent but because we are the stewards of this place. We control this world." And you would begin to think very, very objectively about your situation here.

Even people who claim to be objective and scientific in their perspective are really still governed by this fundamental fear and anxiety.

However, even people who claim to be objective and scientific in their perspective are really still governed by this fundamental fear and anxiety and are still living under the general denial of the fact that the world is being visited and that the Intervention is occurring. They are in such a state of denial that they will not even consider it. They won't come near it. The information, the evidence, is all over the place, but they won't even come near it. They will just say, "Oh, no, no. That's all foolishness. It's just insecure people trying to get attention."

They are in denial. They think they are being reasonable, but really they are being so unreasonable. They are supporting and fortifying their own ignorance and the ignorance of others. And even if they cannot accept that the Intervention is occurring, well, the prospect of life in the Universe is still a very wondrous, romantic journey to them. It is like something that you dream about in the most glorious ways. "Oh, we will meet these advanced races who will give us so much technology and enlighten us on how to live in peace and so forth." This is all foolishness! They have not a clue what is happening out there in the Universe.

If these reasonable people are given a Greater Community perspective, which the teaching in Greater Community Spirituality provides, oh, my God! It touches that core fear and anxiety. And they feel in that moment how utterly vulnerable they are, how undefended they are, how unprepared they are. And you look at people, and they don't have a clue. And they don't want to have a clue. And you look at your world, and you say, "Oh, my God! We could be overtaken without our even knowing it!"

If you did not have the preparation in Greater Community Spirituality, if you did not have anywhere to go with this awareness, it could be overwhelming because you would think that you had no recourse. It is as if humanity, like an unsuspecting native tribe, were just waiting to be taken over by someone else.

Then, of course, there is the problem with the assumption that technology equals salvation. This is becoming a modern religion in many cultures in the world. Developed nations increasingly believe that technology really is their salvation now. There is a problem? Well, technology will solve it. There is something we can't understand? Well, technology will overcome it. There is a situation that could arise for which we are unprepared? Well, technology will meet the challenge. "We will meet the challenge with our technology in the eleventh hour." There is a sort of unquestioned belief that technology is going to save you, regardless of what might happen—technology mixed with human ingenuity, that is. And no matter how overwhelming a situation might be, well, ingenuity plus technology will win the day in the final moments.

Can you see that this is all part of the denial? Wishful thinking is what it is. Regarding the Greater Community, it really is wishful thinking. Do you think humanity is going to generate a technological answer to the presence of Greater Community forces who may want your planet for themselves? We can assure you that it will not be at the level of technology that you will be able to counteract this presence and these influences. Facing a race that is perhaps a thousand years ahead of you technologically, do you think you are going to make a difference in the next few years?

Consider this: The answer will not happen at the level of technology. It will happen at the level of the mind and consciousness. Those who are intervening in the world today are very concerned about preserving the world's resources and about preserving the human presence here as a workforce. They cannot use technology to accomplish this alone. Yes, their technology is useful in neutralizing someone they may want to take for themselves for investigation. However, if they forcefully exert their technology on your world, they will destroy the world's resources and destroy the human presence here, and they cannot do that. Therefore, they must use the very means that you are able to counteract.

Yet here we run into fear again because people realize that without their technology, without the hope and the belief that technology is going to win the day and without human intellect being able to solve the problem, they are back in this very vulnerable place once again. But we are not talking about the intellect here. It is not at the level of the intellect that humanity is going to be able to counteract this presence and to strengthen itself in the Greater Community. The intellect plays a very important role as far as technology goes and in certain kinds of problem solving. But in this situation, it will take a deeper awareness.

> We can assure you that it will not be at the level of technology that you will be able to counteract this presence and these influences.

After all, some of your most intellectually brilliant people are in total denial of the Intervention and think life in the Universe is some distant possibility. And you ask yourself, "Well, if they are so brilliant and so well informed, why can't they feel this presence in the world today? Why can't they even face this as a possibility and study the evidence rather than dismissing it out of hand? If people are so smart, how can they be so stupid?" Ignorance is one thing. Ignorance can be compensated by gaining information and perspective. But this is not merely ignorance. This is arrogance. It is the assumption that *you* know what life is in the Universe. Oh, my God! Humanity knows what life is in the Universe? Oh, my God! Humanity is so far from knowing what life is in the Universe, it is pathetic!

> Some of your most intellectually brilliant people are in total denial of the Intervention and think life in the Universe is some distant possibility.

Given the unfounded belief in technology as the source of human salvation, many people think, well, more technology is more salvation. And they think that technologically advanced races have evolved beyond being self-seeking and contentious and devious. They think that technologically advanced races do not have conflict and that these races have outgrown the chronic problems that humanity still faces. What a ridiculous assumption! You have technology today that your forefathers a hundred years ago could not even imagine. And yet have you overcome these problems yourselves?

Therefore, do not look to the experts to give you the answer. You must find the answer yourself because the experts may not know and may not want to know. Remember, they are human beings just like you and they have their own thresholds of fear and anxiety that they may not be willing to face.

Do not look to the experts to give you the answer. You must find the answer yourself because the experts may not know and may not want to know.

In a way, the Intervention is the most challenging thing that could happen to humanity. Part of humanity's liability or weakness here is its presumption that it really understands life, that it really knows what is happening in the Universe, that it understands who can travel, who cannot travel and how long it takes to get to planets. It assumes that human understanding sets the standard for all understanding in the Universe. This is human arrogance, which supports and fortifies human ignorance.

It is presented in the Teaching in Greater Community Spirituality, and it is presented very boldly in the message from *The Allies of Humanity,* that life in the Universe is challenging, difficult and competitive. And if you approach life in the Universe romantically or if you deny it altogether, you do this at great risk.

What really needs to happen here is a whole new shift in human awareness and human learning. It is as if you have reached this great threshold and there must be a completely new paradigm of understanding. It is not simply that you are building on past understanding, adding another feature or another dimension to human awareness. It is really that you have to make kind of a leap here. This is because human understanding is still so grounded in an anthropocentric view of the Universe, with humanity at the center of everything and the unquestioned belief that life in the Universe functions according to human values and ideals

.For many people, there is still this idea that God is primarily concerned with humanity as the centerpiece of Creation and that everything else is just sort of wallpaper to this great human drama. Look at your religions. Are they really equipped to deal with the realities of the Greater Community? Let me give you this analogy: There are native tribes that have been overtaken and cultures that have been assimilated and destroyed countless places in your world in the last 500 years. It is still occurring today. They have their religions, which can be very expansive. But their religions usually do not include the reality of human life beyond their borders, which puts them in a very vulnerable position because they really don't know how to respond in the face of an Intervention.

Human understanding is still so grounded in an anthropocentric view of the Universe, with humanity at the center of everything and the unquestioned belief that life in the Universe functions according to human values and ideals.

Compared to the Greater Community, humanity's outpost in this world is like a little village in the jungle. And when this village is confronted with forces coming to seek advantages, what can it do? Well, interestingly enough, it can actually do a great deal. The first thing is to become aware of the Intervention and to face your own fear and anxiety. Here it is necessary to see how ill prepared you are, how vulnerable you are and how easily even you could be persuaded to think and to believe that the visitors are here for your benefit. This is the first threshold, a threshold which unfortunately many people will not cross. They will withdraw or go into denial or cast a very preferred perspective over the whole

Look at your religions. Are they really equipped to deal with the realities of the Greater Community?

matter. The first threshold is to recognize your situation. Even if the Intervention were not occurring at this time, you know it would occur at some time.

You see, it's interesting. People have their grand notions of intelligent life in the Universe and advanced technology and other races of altruistic beings out there floating around. Yet the thing that people are most afraid of is that they will encounter others like themselves, but more powerful. What is the thing that people are really afraid of regarding the prospect of encountering intelligent life from beyond the world? They are afraid they will meet themselves. In a different form, perhaps. Perhaps the visitors will look different and use a different language and a different means of communication. But the thing that people are really afraid of, the thing that no one can even talk about, particularly in enlightened circles, is the reality that they are going to meet themselves.

> Compared to the Greater Community, humanity's outpost in this world is like a little village in the jungle.

This is not to suggest that your visitors are human beings or that intelligent life functions according to human ideals and beliefs. What we are really telling you here, and what you must come to terms with, is that you are going to meet beings who are driven by the same needs that you are driven by.

The Greater Community of life in which you live is a very competitive environment. You can see this competition in your own world. You can see it in the natural world. You can see it at the level of plants and animals. Yet the Greater Community is a competitive environment on a scale you cannot even comprehend. This means that everyone who is in that environment, particularly those who are active participants in trade and commerce, must find resources and gain alliances with other nations and often try to persuade those nations to enter into alliances with them.

The need for resources does not end because of technology. Technology does not end the fundamental needs of life. It hasn't for you and it hasn't for anyone in the Universe. Yes, it frees you from certain basic activities, but it creates more complexity. You may not need to go out and hunt and fish for your food, or farm, but you must go to work. You must maintain a much more complicated life in order to afford the food that you need to eat. Technology has freed you from hunting and gathering and has freed you from basic agriculture, but it has not freed you from the need for resources. Indeed, it has made your life more complicated and more exciting, but in other ways, more difficult and more stressful.

It is the same with life in the Universe. Everyone has to eat. Everyone has to maintain what they have created. Everyone must deal with other forms of intelligent life that may be vying or competing for basic resources. Do you think an advanced nation in the Universe does not have a great need for resources?

The larger nations or organizations may become, the more restrictive they will be regarding personal freedom for their constituents, and the greater the need will be for order and conformity. That is why in the Universe the really free nations are small and isolated. Their technology has given them advantages, but they must protect it and keep it hidden.

It would be like you getting a million dollars and going out into the marketplace with your million dollars. Well, what a rude shock. Now everyone is your friend. Now everyone wants to invite you to invest in their endeavor, in their project, or they need your financial help because they are in difficulty. If humanity were ever able to travel beyond its borders and carry its great incentive and enterprise into the Universe, it would be like the little housewife having a million dollars and going out into the marketplace. You would not last very long.

You see, this reality of life, which is so denied, is something that must be faced. Who will you meet in the Universe? You will meet others like you. Not exactly like you. Not looking like you or talking like you or dressing like you. But they are like you in their needs. And those who are resource explorers in the Universe are not the spiritually enlightened.

Therefore, it is necessary to counteract many of the prevailing assumptions and beliefs, fantasies and myths, because otherwise you cannot face the situation. And if you cannot face the situation, it will overtake you. People pray to God for guidance, for strength, for courage and for peace, and God sends Greater Community Spirituality as a preparation. And people say, "What is this? I did not ask for this! What will I do with this? It isn't relevant!" You don't know what's relevant. What you think is relevant may be important to you personally, but it's not going to protect your rights and your freedoms in the future.

Humanity's encounter with intelligent life in the Universe is not the product of human journeys into space or human science or human philosophy or human religion. It is the result

> What you think is relevant may be important to you personally, but it's not going to protect your rights and your freedoms in the future.

of the Intervention. It is the result of other races coming here in order to preserve the world for themselves, believing that humanity will destroy the world in its conflicts, that humanity will ruin the world's valuable resources.

Think about this. This is how people would react. If, let us say, developed nations in the world found some little tribe in the recesses of the jungles who were sitting on tons of gold or other kinds of minerals, or had vast forests full of valuable woods, do you think that the advanced nations would not intervene, particularly if they felt these resources were going to waste? Or how about if the natives were cutting down all the trees because they liked the sunlight or they wanted to grow their own food? Well, the nations of the world would be in there doing everything they could to get the resources, either legally or illegally. That is what human nations would do. Do you think they would sit by and let the natives just despoil or neglect what they have? Of course not. Well, if the land is of no value to the powerful nations, sure, give them their reservation. But if they are sitting on $100 million in gold, that would not be a reservation.

Your world is viewed like that by your visitors and by others in the Universe who see this precious little world and this race of relatively destructive beings destroying its natural resources and violating its natural laws. Do you think this would not produce an Intervention? Some people think, "Well, of course, they would come and ask permission to be here and our nations, our governments would work out a deal." Oh, my God! Are you kidding? What would happen instead is that those intervening races would establish a plan of intervention and integration because they want to preserve the human workforce. They cannot live in your world. They will have you do all the work. Get the natives to mine the gold. Just like what has happened in your world. Do you think the natives' permission is needed? Well, maybe they'll find a way to induce you to give your permission, but they are going to get what they want. In your situation in the world today, your visitors are going to get what they want unless you stop them. And the way you are going to stop them is not merely by using technology. It is by intelligence and by cunning. And by cooperation in the human family.

THE FIRST STEP IN COUNTERACTING THE INTERVENTION IS AWARENESS, BUT THE AWARENESS REALLY IS A BIG THRESHOLD BECAUSE OF PEOPLE'S FEAR, ANXIETY AND FAILED IDEALISM. Can you face your own fear? Can you face your own vulnerability? Can you face the fact that perhaps you have been really wrong in your assessment of the situation, if you have given it any thought at all? People may say, "Well, ok, we get the awareness. Now what's the next thing?" Ha! They don't see that the awareness is really big!

THE NEXT STEP IS YOU HAVE TO CREATE A GREATER COMMUNITY PERSPECTIVE IN THE WAY YOU LOOK AT YOURSELF AND IN THE WAY THAT YOU LOOK AT YOUR WORLD. Do you think humanity would be destroying the resources of the world if it could recognize that preserving and sustaining these resources is the very thing that will preserve human freedom in the future? If humanity loses its ability to sustain itself and becomes dependent upon foreign powers for not just advanced technology but for even basic resources, you will lose your freedom.

Perhaps you may say, "Oh, I don't believe it. We wouldn't lose our freedom." But if you think about it objectively, you will see that you will lose your freedom. Either overtly or subtly, you would become reliant upon other races in the Universe, and they would determine the terms of engagement. They would control your world. Yet because they do not want to create a human revolution, they will attempt to control your world in such a way that it would be acceptable to people to be controlled. That is why the Intervention that is occurring today is so devious and is being carried out so carefully over time. If they came here in force, everyone would just react and there would be huge warfare and the world's resources would be severely damaged. There would be no human workforce here that would be either willing or able to help the intervening races, and the whole project would be spoiled.

You must gain a Greater Community perspective. You are a human being living in this world. This world is unprotected. It is valuable. It is sought by others. Intervention by other races will increase over time. How will you defend your borders? How will you be able to determine who is here and why they are here and what they are doing? This cannot be the privilege of secret groups and secret governments.

Humanity has to grow up and outgrow its childish self-preoccupations. It has to outgrow its adolescent fantasies about itself and about life and become realistic. Otherwise, the Intervention will continue, and your world will gradually become governed by foreign powers. And where will you go then with your complaints, your protest and your outrage? It is for this reason that gaining the awareness and a Greater Community perspective is critical because without these, you cannot even take the next step.

THE THIRD STEP IS LEARNING ABOUT THE MENTAL ENVIRONMENT. The Mental Environment is the arena of influence. People know very little about it, but it is very important in Greater Community interactions, particularly between races or organizations that compete with each other. They have to spend a great deal of time trying to discern what the other is going to do and trying to influence the other in subtle ways. This does not happen through technology as much as it happens through consciousness, through awareness, through the projection of thought and through cunning activities. Competitors generally share the same technology, so technology is not the advantage. The advantage is cunning and persuasion. You cannot see this yet because you are still thinking like you live in isolation and that the Universe is governed by human principles. You do not want to think about this because you realize that you do not have these skills. And that makes you feel afraid and vulnerable. So the third step in preparation is developing skill in the Mental Environment. You can actually learn how to do this, but you must have the awareness and you must have a Greater Community perspective to start.

THE FOURTH THING WHICH REALLY MUST BE DEVELOPED ALL ALONG IS KNOWLEDGE. What is Knowledge? When we speak of Knowledge, we are not talking about perspective or bodies of information or data. We are talking about the ability to know— beyond deception, beyond appearances, beyond personal preference, beyond fear and beyond denial. The ability to *know*. The Intervention has been going on actively for almost 50 years. And people who claim to be studying the UFO phenomenon, well, do they know anything yet, or are they still gathering data? "Well, we don't want to come to any premature conclusions. You know, this is so complicated and we may never understand it!" What are you talking about? Is this denial? Is this the unwillingness to come to a conclusion? Or is it that people simply just don't know? Can't they see and feel what this really is? After 50 years, can't they see and feel what this really is? They need more evidence? Oh, my God! How much more evidence? Another 50 years of evidence? A hundred years of evidence? 50 more years of evidence, and it will be all over then. And the conclusion you will come to will be so obvious.

It is like the person in a 30-year marriage who never should have gotten married anyway, and it takes them 30 years to figure out that really they made a mistake somewhere back there, and they really should have followed their deeper feelings and not walked down the aisle with this other person. But they have been trying to make it all right for the last 30 years.

Without Knowledge, you will only know what others want you to know. You will only think what others want you to think—whether it be your parents, your culture, your social group, your government, or the Greater Community. You will basically be like cattle and you will be led around, from pasture to pasture. Without Knowledge, the Mental Environment overtakes you and overwhelms you. Knowledge is the deeper Spiritual Mind within you. It is the only part of you that is unaffected by the Mental Environment. It is the only part of you that is free from deception and manipulation.

Do you want freedom for yourself? Then you must learn the way of Knowledge. Otherwise, what is freedom? Having more money? Working less, having more money? Is that freedom? Look at the wealthy who have no freedom. Oh, they have lots of money, and they can go anywhere they want. They do not even have to work, some of them. Are they free? Or are they slaves to their money and their situation and their privileges and their appetites and their fears?

The message in *The Allies of Humanity Briefings* is about freedom. And to have freedom, you must become aware of the Intervention. You must gain a Greater Community perspective. You must learn about the Mental Environment and its impact upon you. And you must develop your experience of Knowledge. Not a lot of technology here though technology may play a small role in all of this.

Without Knowledge, you will only know what others want you to know. You will only think what others want you to think.

When we speak about learning the way of Knowledge, we are not talking about just developing intuition. That is not adequate. You must actually connect with the Knowing Mind within yourself, and this is not an easy task. There will be many who will be unwilling or unable to do this. But not everyone has to do this in order for humanity to turn the tide, to develop a Greater Community awareness and to begin to build boundaries around your world.

Force cannot be used to take over a planet like yours. Therefore, the Intervention must be subtle. It must be deceptive. It must be invasive. It cannot use brute force. This is good for you because you could not withstand brute force. And brute force would destroy the outcome for the visitors, if you can call them visitors. There are many reasons why they will not use it.

The Creator has responded to this great need of humanity,

a need that is barely even recognized as a need, by presenting the teaching in Greater Community Spirituality. This teaching encompasses the reality of life in the Greater Community. Never has such a teaching been given in the world before because it was not needed before. Yes, there are many spiritual teachings that emphasize the way of Knowledge to a certain degree. But a Greater Community way of Knowledge has never been given in the world before. You need it now, however. It will not replace the world's religions but instead give them a greater scope, a greater perspective, and a greater context in which to continue to grow, to exist and to evolve.

Yet it is curious that the world's religious leaders will perhaps be the most resistant to learning a Greater Community Spirituality. To preserve their traditions, their authority and their power, they will perhaps deny the very thing that will give their tradition a future in the Greater Community. For without human freedom, there is no future. Without human self-determination, there is no future. And without an understanding of the Greater Community, there is no future for anyone here, not a future that you could embrace anyway.

> The Creator has responded to this great need of humanity, a need that is barely even recognized as a need.

You must see the relevance of this to yourself. All that you want out of life, all that you want to be, do and have, the Intervention could take it all away from you. Are you going to mindlessly pursue your personal goals and to hell with everything else, saying it doesn't matter?

Even if the Intervention were not happening, the degradation of your natural resources and the growing population of the world would change what is available to you anyway. Some people say, "Well, I'm just going to go get what I want, and I'm not going to worry about anything else." When people think like that, they are like locusts. Thrown upon the land, they are going to consume everything in sight. And they will leave a wasteland and move on until there is nowhere to move on to, and then they will all die out. Is this the promise for human advancement? To be like parasites that destroy the host and when the host dies, they all die too?

Now, most people would say, "Of course not! Absolutely not!" But if their behavior is self-seeking, then this is an appropriate analogy. Interestingly enough, those who are intervening in your world view humanity as a sort of destructive force in the world that is going to destroy this fabulous place. Their attitude is, "We're going to get in there and stop them. And if they can't use their world properly and preserve it, well, we'll save it for ourselves. They can work for us." This is exactly how they think. This is their perspective. This is how you would think if you were in their place. Even with all of humanity's great idealism, you would think like this too. "We are not going to let them destroy this place! If they can't benefit from it, we will!" This is exactly how a human government would respond. Perhaps this is how you personally would respond.

Those intervening are not evil. They simply see the situation from a certain perspective. They are not guided by Knowledge or spirituality, or they would not be intervening here.

There are people in the world who want the Intervention because they think that the alien races here will somehow save humanity from itself. They believe in the same perspective as the alien races themselves. Sometimes they reach this conclusion within themselves. Sometimes this thinking is encouraged through the Intervention. Yet the result is the same—loss of human freedom and self-determination, which will be very complete. If you think about this, you will realize that this is the worst possible scenario for you.

This is why the Creator is providing the preparation for the Greater Community. This is why it must be learned and taken to heart. This is why the awareness must be gained. People must face their fear and anxiety and realize the situation they are in. They must gain a new understanding of where they stand in the Universe and their role and responsibility as the native peoples and stewards of this world. They must exercise the power that they have individually and collectively to preserve their own native grounds.

There are people in the world who want the Intervention because they think that the alien races here will somehow save humanity from itself.

Your spiritual understanding needs to change for you to realize what God has given humanity to preserve the advancement of human freedom, understanding and cooperation. In the Universe, these must be defended. You need to recognize that you have to outgrow your fantasies and your ideals, even your demands and expectations, to see the situation clearly. The Creator has asked the allies of humanity to be observers, to provide commentary and to present their message so that humanity can begin to gain a Greater Community perspective.

God has given a teaching about the Mental Environment and Knowledge. Learning the way of Knowledge is an individual spiritual journey for each person. Knowledge is the greater intelligence that lives within you. It knows how to deal with the Greater Community. Knowledge is not governed by human beliefs, assumptions, preoccupations, deceptions, ideals or ambitions. It is pure. It is the holy part of you. It knows. Your mind thinks. Knowledge knows. The gulf between them seems great, but they can be united together. And this is the ultimate goal of your spiritual development. This gift of Greater Community Spirituality is meant to give human freedom a real foundation, to empower the individual, to empower the group, to empower humanity, which is losing power every day to those who are intervening in the world.

> Your spiritual understanding needs to change for you to realize what God has given humanity to preserve the advancement of human freedom, understanding and cooperation.

We hope this discourse provides clarity, but it is really only the first step. Do not think you can read this discourse or read *The Allies of Humanity Briefings* and say, "Well, I understand now. I know what to do." You do not yet know what to do. But you may be beginning to gain an understanding. If this stirs something within you deeply, then Knowledge within you is being activated. But there is much to learn ahead.

> Knowledge is not governed by human beliefs, assumptions, preoccupations, deceptions, ideals or ambitions. It is pure. It is the holy part of you. It knows. Your mind thinks. Knowledge knows.

Humanity's encounter with the realities of life beyond this world is a new threshold, perhaps the greatest threshold that humanity has ever faced. The learning will have to be rapid. Do not think you already know or understand. You do not. You may have an idea. You may experience a resonance with this message. You may feel it is important, but you still have to train and prepare.

You don't climb the highest mountain in the world because you love mountains. You don't climb the highest mountain in the world because you have hiking boots. You have to train and prepare, or you won't make it.

This is the challenge of your time. This is the greatness of your time. This is where you will find your own greatness. You will never find your greatness in your individual pursuits, for there is no greatness there. You will only find your greatness in responding to a real need in the world and to the calling that lives within you even at this moment. This is the great situation that will bring out the greatness in you, if you can respond.

You will only find your greatness in responding to a real need in the world and to the calling that lives within you even at this moment.

Effects of the Pacification Program

It is easy to ask questions. It is more difficult to find the real answers. People are hungry for answers, but they do not have the awareness yet. So when considering the message in *The Allies Briefings*, people must begin to develop a Greater Community awareness and sensitivity. Just getting answers to questions does not develop this awareness or sensitivity. And indeed, even if you have the right answer, if you cannot experience it, if you cannot recognize it, if you cannot see its application, well, what good is it? It is lost on the person who is asking.

Therefore, it always comes back to developing the awareness and sensitivity and the ability to know. People want proof, and so they go to whoever they think is the expert, and the expert gives their opinions, and people say, "Ah! This must be the proof because the expert said so." But it is all opinions. Without Knowledge, everything is just opinions in the mind. And these opinions are developed by people's conditioning, by their attitudes and by their temperament. People can experience something and make conclusions and evaluations but be completely wrong in their estimation.

However, we are talking about higher consciousness here. We are not talking about having answers. Answers, without this higher consciousness, will not be enough, and their application will not be understood. Ultimately, you must gain this higher consciousness. This consciousness transcends human culture, human conditioning and even your biological identity. It is an awareness of life as it is moving all around you and through everything else. You need this higher consciousness to understand the plants and the animals, the weather and the movement of the world. You need this to understand the presence of negative forces in the Mental Environment and the presence of the Angelic Forces, which are here to serve you. And certainly, you must have this consciousness to be aware of the Greater Community forces in the world, to recognize their manifestations, their intentions and their methods. You need this higher awareness to tell friend from foe.

> We are talking about higher consciousness here. We are not talking about having answers. Answers, without this higher consciousness, will not be enough.

So when people ask a lot of questions, the real answer is the development of higher consciousness. This leads you into the mystery, where you may not be willing to go, but this is where you must go if you are going to understand. This is the mystery of your life—the mystery of what you know, the mystery of who you are, the mystery of why you are here and the mystery of what you must respond to. You are not here simply to fill your mind with more answers that cannot be recognized or understood.

This, then, moves things in the right direction. Yet of course there are people who cannot tolerate the mystery and must have answers, thinking answers will resolve their inquiry. These people will constitute the majority of people who inquire about *The Allies Briefings* and who will question you about it. You, personally, cannot answer all the questions there are about the Allies—who they are, where they come from, how they got here, their method of propulsion, where they are hiding and how they communicate. How can you possibly answer all these questions?

However, you can be aware of the Allies, and you have the ability to recognize the validity of their message. You have learned enough about life and about nature to understand their point of view and what they emphasize and why it is necessary. This is because of higher consciousness, not because you have answers. *The Allies of Humanity Briefings* promote questions. The reason they don't answer every question is because you must develop the higher consciousness. If they told the reader everything about themselves, people would say, "Huh, I don't believe it! Marshall's making it all up!" You see, without the higher consciousness, people cannot make a connection.

> You are not here simply to fill your mind with more answers that cannot be recognized or understood.

Already you can see the effects of the Pacification Program that is being generated by the Intervention. There are already many people who have fallen prey to this, either by their own inclinations or by outside influence. Here people are led to believe that they can not really judge anything. "Well, I don't want to be negative. I'll be open to it." Who told them to be open to it? "I'll be open to whatever happens." Who told them to be open to whatever happens? People's critical discernment is being destroyed. So something happens and they say, "Well, you know, I don't want to judge the situation." What are you talking about! You need to evaluate what is happening. These people think they cannot be critical. "Well, I can't really be critical. I don't want to be negative." Well, it may be necessary to speak out and say that something is really not appropriate. But these people can't even do that. People who have been affected by this Pacification Program cannot even make a decision. They cannot look at anything and say, "Well, this is a good thing," or "This is really not a good thing for me." So they welcome everything, thinking that is how you must be with life.

Already you can see the effects of the Pacification Program that is being generated by the Intervention.

That is not how you must be with life. It is true you must be willing to look at everything. But it is not true that you must accept everything, bond with everything, welcome everything. Of course not! Higher consciousness does not mean that you do not make critical evaluations. It simply means you view things from a higher vantage point. This does not mean that everything becomes gray. It means that everything becomes clear. You clearly see what to do and what not to do, what is good and what is not good. If this is not the product of spiritual study, then someone is being disabled.

While it is true you must learn not to judge a situation based upon your conditioning or beliefs, ultimately you must judge a situation based upon Knowledge, the Spiritual Intelligence that lives within you. This is the final arbiter in your discernment.

However, people do not recognize this. They take the first step and they think it is the last step. The first step is where you do not judge. This means you must learn to look and recognize something, which you cannot do if you judge it immediately. This is the first step, but people think it is the last step. The last step is very different from the first step. You do not judge in the moment because you need to see and know and recognize what you are looking at. This is discernment. You cannot be discerning if you judge things outright. Yet beyond this discernment, you must see clearly if something is good or not.

So you may recognize that the Intervention really is not good for humanity. In itself, the Intervention is not a good thing! But if you say, "Oh, I cannot judge the situation," how will you ever know? You may want to think, "Well, it's probably good at some other level." A pacified person will say, "I will see how it is good for us because everything that happens is good for us." This is not only human ignorance; this demonstrates the effects of the Pacification Program, which encourages people to trust things unwittingly, without discernment.

Higher consciousness does not mean that you do not make critical evaluations. It simply means you view things from a higher vantage point.

You can see this everywhere. You can see it in the UFO community. You can see it in spiritual communities. You can see it emerging in people all around you. *The Allies Briefings* will create a stir because they advocate discernment. They say, "The Intervention is not good for you." Yet many people say, "Well, I don't know. It must be good. I mean, it can't be bad." They're befuddled. They don't know what to think. "Well, I don't know. I can't really come to any decisions about it." What are you talking about? Has your decision making become disabled? And if so, who disabled it? Why are some people thinking they must be open to everything and receptive to everything? Yes, they want to be non-judgmental, but that is only the first step. They don't take the next step. They don't exercise discernment. In some cases, their discernment has fallen away.

This is a critical problem. As a result of this Pacification Program, people cannot see and cannot know, and basically, though they are confused and frightened perhaps, they will just go along. "Well, I'll just go along. I'll just try to accept what is happening in my life." People who are pacified can't resist. They can't fight against something because they don't think it's all right to do that. They think that everything has to be embraced. Where did this come from?

These ideas of unquestioned acceptance are prevalent in much of the spiritual teaching you see today. And people accept these ideas wholeheartedly. They think, "Well, this is the higher truth. We follow the higher truth." Consider this in the light of the Pacification Program and you will begin to see how pervasive it really is.

People who are being pacified will be led to believe that they are gaining higher consciousness when in fact all of their power is being taken away from them. The Pacification Program is based upon an understanding of human psychology and human tendencies. Here people are conditioned to think that in order to be acceptable to God, they must basically give away what God has given them to use. "Well, to be acceptable to

The Pacification Program, encourages people to trust things unwittingly, without discernment.

People who are pacified can't resist. They can't fight against something because they don't think it's all right to do that.

God, I must be meek and mild and non-judgmental and all-embracing of everything. I will look for the good in everything."

Where did this come from? Is such acquiescence purely a human invention? Is this something that people just concoct for themselves in order to be happy in the moment? Well, in some cases, this is true. But consider the pacification of humanity. How are people pacified? They are told what they want to hear, and they are told they don't really need to consider anything else. After all, if everything that happens to you is good, then why resist anything? Just embrace it all! This is the Pacification Program at work.

This influence is becoming omnipresent around you. People flock to places where the Intervention is operating, thinking that the "energy" there is so high. They say, "This is such an enlightening place." Oh, my God! They are jumping into the fire. They are giving themselves away wholeheartedly. They go to these places and they feel the energy there, and they think, "Oh, this is really a powerful place. This is where it is happening!" And the longer they stay, the less they know, and the less they think they can return to their former lives. They become ever more listless and self-involved, and they become ever more dysfunctional.

People who are being pacified will be led to believe that they are gaining higher consciousness when in fact all of their power is being taken away from them.

This disengagement produces an anxiety at a deeper level, a level where you know that your life is not progressing and that you are not going where you need to go. Yet these people will think that this discomfort is part of their fear, or part of their psychology that must be eradicated and exorcised out of themselves. And so they will work hard to ignore the very signs that are telling them that their lives are amiss and that they are losing their lives.

They will say, "All is love. Just be loving. There is only love." If they knew what they were talking about, actually that would be true. But they think love is simply passivity, happiness and acquiescence because that is the Pacification Program working on them. Now they are extending it to other people and becoming pacifiers

> People flock to places where the Intervention is operating, thinking that the "energy" there is so high.

themselves. And after awhile, well, they will not know what they know. And if something is really wrong, they will feel discomfort, but they will think it is just part of their psychological problem, and they will try to overlook it or remove it or bury it. And then they will do whatever is told them to do by the Intervention. They will say, "Oh, I got a message. I have to go do this. I am being guided. This is inner guidance for me."

It will be very hard to awaken people from this. You have to awaken yourself first. People are so immersed in their listlessness and their pursuit of happiness, it's almost like they are beyond reach. They are so lulled and so conditioned, you would have to drop a bomb in their laps to wake them up!

You can see the effects of the Pacification Program in spiritual communities in many places. Certainly not to all people, but to many people, acquiescence looks like the easy path, the easy way, the way to true happiness. Give up knowing anything, give up evaluating anything, give up resisting anything, and it looks like, "Oh, everything is just happiness from now on. Smooth sailing ahead!"

These nice people, the Intervention will simply lull them into a listless state and then basically they will not be a problem, and they will be receptive to whatever is given them. Their natural knowing will be so removed from their awareness, it will become the enemy now. They will think it is fearfulness. They will think it is negativity. And they will not want any part of it.

This is actually happening now. We are talking about an extreme case, but these extreme cases are growing in scope and magnitude. Many more people are simply falling into this state—even the young people, some of whom are especially prone to this kind of conditioning.

Consider this. True happiness comes from being true to yourself, from developing your own integrity and from living honorably with your integrity. True relationships are based upon sharing real integrity with others, building relationships of integrity, relationships that express your deeper nature and purpose in life.

> People are so immersed in their listlessness and their pursuit of happiness, it's almost like they are beyond reach.

However, look at the relationships of a pacified person, who says, "Well, we're together as long as it feels good, as long as it's okay, and if we're not together, it's okay, and whatever we do is okay." But it's not okay. And they know it's not okay, but their natural knowing has been removed from their awareness. As a result, they say, "I will not feel those things. They disrupt my happiness, my peace, my equanimity." And yet there is no peace or equanimity because there is no integrity, and because there is no integrity, there is no real relationship.

Do you see here how the poison is immersed in the very food that people want to eat? Spiritual food is being poisoned.

How many spiritual teachers today are teaching real discernment? How many are promoting real personal integrity? How many are encouraging people to look clearly and see? How many teachers are encouraging their students to respond to the world? There are indeed some, but look around and you will see the Pacification Program being promoted unknowingly.

How perfect this is for the alien agenda. It takes time, but from their perspective, well, the results are worth it. The Intervention will then have a vast network of compliant people through which their agenda can flow. And the people will never know where it is coming from.

In another scenario, the situation becomes more complicated. Here the Intervention begins to show its darker side. Not everyone can be easily pacified. Those who cannot be pacified by the Intervention will be directed by the Intervention to judge those who oppose it. This will be particularly true for people who have extreme religious views and prejudices. These people will be directed to condemn those who do not share their views. Indeed, there are people in some religious communities who will receive messages that all the enemies of Christ must be eradicated if they cannot be saved and that the Second Coming will require the cleansing of the human family.

There are individuals today who are being so directed, and though they do not necessarily represent the leadership of these religious communities, their emphasis will grow as their frustration grows. They are waiting for the great arrival of Jesus, and they think it is not happening because of the sinfulness of the human family, sinfulness that must now be eradicated and not simply resisted. And the Jesus who will come will not be the real Jesus, but will be the Jesus prepared through the Intervention. This will be a false Jesus that they cannot really recognize because they are not developed in Knowledge. This Jesus will not bring peace but a reckoning. This reckoning will be welcomed by the followers because they are full of grievances themselves and believe that their prophecies are not being fulfilled because of the sinfulness of humanity and that this sinfulness must now be removed in order to bring Heaven on Earth.

Can you see for a moment how easy it would be for a Greater Community presence here, the Intervention, so skillful in influencing the Mental Environment and so aware of human tendencies and frailties, to provide this kind of influence? Can you see how, because of this manipulation, the righteous could begin to wage war against those people who disagree with them and against those who would preserve Knowledge in the world? Can you see how easy it would be for this to be generated?

> The Intervention will then have a vast network of compliant people through which their agenda can flow. And the people will never know where it is coming from.

Even the true believers in Christ would be targeted, for they do not share these grievances, and thus they are not in conformity with those individuals who are being directed by the Intervention. True believers in Christ would emphasize harmony and recognition and tolerance. But those being directed by the Intervention only want revenge for their failed prophecies. They want God's punishment to be exacted, and they are willing to be the executioners. They are willing to be the judge and the jury to carry out what they believe now is God's will. How will the Intervention eradicate its opponents? Should it gain enough power, you can see how this can be done.

Where pacification cannot be achieved, the Intervention will influence people to carry out their hostilities upon one another. As the world becomes more difficult, as resources diminish, as populations grow, as competition increases, as tragedy occurs more frequently, people's sense of tolerance will diminish, and their grievances will be encouraged—not only by the Intervention, but certainly by those people who are ambitious and want to put themselves in positions of power. How perfectly this falls into the alien agenda, which seeks to simplify and restructure human allegiance. The Intervention does not care what religion they use so long as it can achieve these results. That is why a devout Christian, Muslim, Hindu or Buddhist must all learn the Way of Knowledge. Otherwise, how could they tell the difference between a spiritual influence and a Greater Community influence? To the undiscerning, well, it all looks like it's coming from a higher place, from the Heavens. Who, then, can you trust?

The Intervention can create wonderful spiritual scenarios to activate those individuals who are most prone to be their messengers. It is not difficult for the Intervention to do. They simply stage a drama and put someone in the middle of it, and this person cannot tell the difference. People do not know what a Greater Community presence is. To them, it is all coming from somewhere else, not at their level, but from a higher place. So, in one scenario, an image of Jesus is projected to a zealous person, and the zealous person says, "Jesus has come to me." And the Jesus says, "You must gather my true followers and you must denounce all others!" And the zealous follower says, "Yes, Master, yes, Master!"

Incredible? Yes. Impossible? No. If the alien agenda is to create a unified and compliant human allegiance, it must eradicate the dissident elements, the non-compliant elements. They will not do this themselves because then everyone will know that there is an Intervention. Instead, they will have human beings do it for them in the name of people's religious convictions and prejudices. And no one will know what is behind it all. Some people will think it is Satan or Lucifer, but they will not know.

It is humanity's ignorance that is its greatest weakness. It is humanity's Knowledge that is its greatest strength. The Greater Community, the inhabited Universe in which you live, is a very sophisticated environment of interaction and influence. If human beings are going to follow their prejudices, their hatreds and their grievances and cannot tell the difference between a spiritual and a Greater Community influence, then the Greater Community is an extremely hazardous environment. Someone in the Greater Community will eventually win you over to their Collective or to their cause. How will they do this? They will simply use what you already believe in rather than teaching you something new.

> It is humanity's ignorance that is its greatest weakness. It is humanity's Knowledge that is its greatest strength.

This is why learning the Way of Knowledge is so vitally important because this teaches you about the reality of life and spirituality in the Greater Community. It teaches you about the nature of manipulation and how to safeguard yourself and others. It teaches you how to recognize the effects and the manifestations of the Pacification Program and what you can do today to develop your own immunity to these forces, which are so influential on other people.

This is vitally needed in the world today. Every day men and women of good conscience are falling under persuasion that they cannot discern. It is a gradual process. But eventually they end up not even having a clue about what is happening in their lives and being hostile to any kind of correction.

> If happiness is the goal of your life, you will give in. You will compromise your integrity. You will deny your own anxieties. You will overlook the signs and the flags and the clues.

As you begin to develop this Greater Community awareness yourself and to share the Allies' message with others, you will see this resistance. You will see people's inability to respond. It's like someone has pulled the plug within them and now they just don't know anything. And if they do respond at some level, they may try to pacify themselves. They will say, "Well, it's just one point of view, and you know, we have to look for the good in this situation. We really have to embrace this situation. If the visitors are here, then they must be here for a purpose, and we have to open ourselves to this purpose. Maybe some of them are not good, but some of them are, and we have to love them to understand them."

> Those who resist the Intervention will be accused of being unenlightened and fearful.

This is all pacification mentality. This is the easy thing to do. Just give in. And if happiness is the goal of your life, you will give in. You will compromise your integrity. You will deny your own anxieties. You will overlook the signs and the flags and the clues that tell you that something is not right here. You may tell yourself, "Well, it is all just part of the drama of life, and I will be above it all."

Throughout the world today, the Wise are retreating because the Intervention is here. Only a few are in a position to advocate. Marshall is one of those people. Yet he will need others to help him. The world has not been lost. But the risk of it being lost is increasing.

Therefore, you cannot simply retreat and go live the rural pastoral life somewhere, tuning it all out, just being happy every day, going back to nature, carrying the water jugs, planting the corn, cooking the meals and living through the seasons. That is over! If you are going to be conscious, self-determined and have your own integrity, there is no running away now. There is no heading for the woods and pretending it's not happening.

There is no more constant therapy on oneself. In the end, the only real therapy is to become real with what you know, to stand for what you know, to learn the wisdom necessary to carry what you know and to communicate what you know compassionately and powerfully. This is what any form of real therapy must lead to. Are you going to go back and repair your childhood? Are you going to find the unrequited love that your parents did not give you? People who become too concentrated on these things become disabled. They become wheelchair bound in their own minds. They could all become advocates for the truth, but instead, all they become is advocates for therapy, and not a great deal of therapy done today leads to the truth. There is no running away. There is no fulfilling yourself personally at the expense of establishing your own integrity, knowing the truth and standing for the truth.

Humanity must become united, or it will be dominated in the Greater Community. This is so obvious when you think about it. If other forces beyond your world want your planet, its resources and human allegiance, well, if the human family is divided, you are really inviting others to move in on you. "Sure, come on! There is plenty of room for everyone!"

Those who resist the Intervention will be accused of being unenlightened and fearful. Some will be accused of resisting the Intervention to protect their special interests. And there are some people who will resist the Intervention for these interests. However, there are those who will resist the Intervention *because* it is an Intervention. But with the Pacification Program, who can even call it for what it is? Who can say, "This is what it is!" without incurring resistance and condemnation? This is a real problem today.

We encourage the development of people's discernment, discretion and the application of their critical faculties. What we encourage here is not based upon personal prejudice or social conditioning, but upon Knowledge. Knowledge is the part of you that *knows*. It is the greater mind within you that the Creator has given to you to meet the challenges and opportunities of your life. It is the voice of conscience within you. People compare their belief systems and judge each other, but this is not what we are talking about.

We are talking about rescuing humanity from a situation which would enslave it. We are talking about preserving human freedom and self-determination and encouraging human integrity in the midst of forces from the Greater Community who are intervening in your world. Is achieving this impossible? Well, in a way, the truth always looks impossible. The promotion and preservation of the truth always looks like it's facing insurmountable odds. But that is only because the truth is not valued, recognized and felt deeply by enough people. What will get humanity out of this predicament is the same thing that will get humanity out of every predicament. It is facing the truth and doing what needs to be done.

There are many people in the world today who are very uncomfortable because they know that something really wrong is happening. Perhaps they think that their discomfort is just their own psychological problem. Perhaps they think it is a political, economic or environmental problem alone. If they do not have a Greater Community awareness, then they have to focus their attention on something else and look for some other kind of cause. But they know that something is not right about what is happening today. Things don't feel right. Things are moving in a direction that they should not be moving in. Something is going on that is going to change things, but not in a good way. And the people who feel this are uncomfortable. They wake up with this discomfort; they go to bed with this discomfort. It's just there. They feel it when they are out in the world. Something is not right.

Where does this discomfort come from? Why is it there? You can meditate. You can go on vacation. You can have nice food. And you can have moments of delight. But then you

> What will get humanity out of this predicament is the same thing that will get humanity out of every predicament. It is facing the truth and doing what needs to be done.

return to the discomfort. Something is amiss. It's not simply because there is poverty or war or deprivation in the world. These have always been with you. Something else is going on here. Something else is really not right.

Yet you look around and most people are oblivious. They don't know it. They don't feel it. And they don't care. Or they have good excuses. "Well, you know. It's just human nature," or "You know, it's people's fear. They just need to be more loving." And you hear really lame excuses for something that is tremendous.

> The light of truth must become strong because there are greater forces of darkness here now.

Your awareness needs to grow. Your fire needs to grow and become stronger—the fire of truth, the fire of Knowledge. Otherwise, your fire is always snuffed out, extinguished by personal ambivalence, personal fear, personal preference or the kind of listlessness that is the product of the Pacification Program.

The light of truth must become strong because there are greater forces of darkness here now. The deception is deep and complex. The denial is pervasive, and the acquiescence is pervasive and growing more so every day. Only Knowledge within you can penetrate it.

Humanity is losing its freedom, slowly but surely, and in such a way that this loss will be very complete because of the cleverness of the agenda behind it. This can happen because of the predispositions of so many people today. This can happen because of the effects of the Pacification Program, which is so well established now in many parts of the world.

Therefore, it will take courage and a strong advocacy to

activate those people who already feel the discomfort, who already feel the problem but cannot identify it or its source. And it will take a strong advocacy to reach those people who have begun to acquiesce but whose sense of integrity is intact enough that they know that there is a problem within them and around them and who are struggling to maintain their clarity of mind as the fog descends.

For those who have acquiesced completely, there may be no answer. They may be beyond your reach. It would take a Greater Power, the Angelic Presence, to reach them. But even here, it is quite difficult because the pacification can become so complete that people will think that the very hand of Grace that is trying to rescue them is the very thing they must avoid.

You can only reach those who are uncomfortable, who have a sense of knowing that their integrity is being violated and who have begun to feel the persuasion of the Intervention but have not acquiesced to it. There are many people in this camp. You are not speaking to a minority. This advocacy will take time. It is not something that can be done in a few weeks, months or years. It is something that must be continuous.

Humanity's emergence into the Greater Community will be quite difficult because of the Intervention. It will require that a higher consciousness be cultivated, protected and maintained in enough people. It is going to require a greater level of discernment and discretion, greater care about who you associate with and what you communicate. It is going to require a greater awareness and sensitivity to the world and to those forces who are in the world now casting an influence over humanity.

Developing this awareness and this sensitivity and establishing one's personal integrity and relationships that represent this integrity are absolutely fundamental for success. This is what will keep Knowledge alive in the world. This is what will build freedom and keep it alive in the world. This is what will keep humanity intact. For once you lose your integrity and your freedom, it is very difficult to regain them. Very difficult. Even when people have sacrificed their integrity for relationships or for money or for advantage, even under these more normal circumstances, it is very difficult to regain it. You have to mount tremendous effort and take risks. It is easier, then, to stay out of trouble than it is to get out. You do not want to become a prisoner in your own world. You do not want to become a prisoner in your own mind. You do not want to become a prisoner to anyone or anything else.

If you could have a Greater Community perspective in these matters, you would recognize that though humanity has great difficulties and serious weaknesses, it is still relatively free in the Universe. Of course, living on the surface of your world in isolation, you cannot see this because you do not have the perspective. That is why *The Allies Briefings* are so valuable, because they give you a perspective that you yourself could not otherwise have. How could you compare yourself to the rest of life in the Universe? How could you understand the value of your freedom if you could not see that freedom like this is rare and must be protected well in the Greater Community?

This is why the Allies provide a greater perspective. Yet some people will complain, "Well, they do not give us answers. They do not tell us dates and facts and figures and locations." That is not what is important. It is the understanding, the perspective, the higher consciousness that are critically important. Who cares where the Allies come from? The names of their worlds would be meaningless to you. You are not going to be able to go there for so long! Certainly not in your lifetime. The Allies are providing what is important for you to know about the Greater Community and about the Intervention. They are telling you who is here, why they are here and what they are doing. They are pointing the way to what must be done to counteract this Intervention, which includes the development of Greater Community awareness and a higher consciousness.

This development must be emphasized always. It is so vitally important, or people will miss the whole point. They will just assume that this is merely some phenomenal thing that probably isn't true anyway. Some will say, "These Allies don't even tell us their names or how they got here." This is stupidity! If God sends an emissary, do you deny the emissary because he does not answer trivial questions? God has sent the Allies here to help educate humanity and to warn humanity of the grave risks that it faces at this time. Is this going to be denied because some trivial information is not provided?

This is why the development of Greater Community awareness is vitally important now. This is why higher consciousness must be promoted and preserved. This is why you keep Knowledge alive in the world. It is this that must be supported and honored at this great turning point.

Honor this material. Recognize it as being a gift of Grace. Respond to it. Have the courage to do this. Resist the pacification. Resist the influence to become listless and unresponsive to your own Knowledge. Resist the temptation to devote yourself to your own happiness above and beyond everything else. Resist the temptation to attack people of other faiths, cultures or nations. Resist the Intervention through awareness, through advocacy, through understanding. Promote human cooperation, unity and integrity.

Understanding the Intervention

The *Allies of Humanity Briefings* will arouse many questions. This is good because these questions must be asked and considered. It is not merely that answers should be readily given, but that the questions be deeply considered and that the questioners think for themselves what the answers could possibly be.

If humanity is ever to become strong and self-determined within the Greater Community, then it must have more people who can think independently and critically and consider things deeply.

The Allies themselves will remain mysterious. For some people, this will be difficult, but it must be this way, for the Allies really are spying on the Intervention, and to protect themselves, the Allies must remain hidden.

The Allies themselves will not divulge much information about their origin, their identities and so forth. They claim that this information would be meaningless to people, but really the greater reason for this is that the Allies want to maintain their anonymity. This anonymity protects them and their sources.

It is perhaps difficult to accept these things at first

because people do not understand the difficulties of life in the Greater Community. They do not understand how Knowledge must be transmitted from one race to another, particularly when there is a situation like an Intervention underway. In a manner of speaking, humanity is under siege, though perhaps this seems too strong a word because the activities of the "visitors" seem so subtle and evasive. But given the results of this Intervention, the word "siege" here really is appropriate. If you try to help another nation that is under siege and you want to remain hidden, then you have to protect yourself and your sources and communicate in such a way that the message can be dispensed effectively with minimum risk of the information being destroyed or corrupted in any way.

This is why the message is being given to one person. If it were given to many people, they could perhaps misinterpret it, and they would have different versions of what they had been given, and then they would contend with each other, and the whole message could be lost or corrupted. As long as this one person can continue to receive the information, and if he has enough support around him, then this is the best protection against misunderstanding and against conflict arising. Since this is information that humanity cannot gain on its own, it must be delivered by those in the Greater Community who are attempting to help you and who are concerned about your freedom in the future.

How can humanity on its own understand the intricacies of relations in the Greater Community? This is not possible. And if any attempt were made to explain these things, well, it would seem fantastic, and people would have no way of verifying it for themselves, unless of course they were strong with Knowledge.

Therefore, the Allies will remain mysterious. Some people will understand this. Some people will not understand this. The Allies cannot reveal much about their own history beyond what they have told you in the Briefings. Some people can accept this. Others will become suspicious. But what we are really talking about here is discretion. You do not reveal everything to people at the outset when they can barely understand or accept your initial offerings. Their first questions must go unanswered because they do not have enough trust in their contact, and they do not have enough trust in their own Knowledge, the Spiritual Intelligence within them, to be able to discern what is true and what is not true.

Because there is so little honesty in the world, what is truly honest will be suspected and will be considered devious, especially by those who are devious themselves. It is, in fact, very difficult to present something pure to the world without it being defiled or compromised, even at the outset. The one person chosen to receive these messages is chosen because he has no position in the world, because he has no social standing and because he has been well prepared for this. Yes, he will have questions, and he does. Yes, he will be afraid of certain things, and he has been. But as long as he can receive the message and present it in a pure form, whether he himself can fully understand it or not, that is the important thing. Because the message is in a pure form and does not conform to people's expectations, preferences or beliefs, at the outset not

> The Allies will remain mysterious. Some people will understand this. Some people will not understand this.

everyone will be able to comprehend it. And there will be much discussion and much suspicion, and many fears will be projected upon it, particularly by people whose previous understanding is challenged in any way by this new revelation.

Obviously, people would want the Allies to be many things. They would want the Allies to be saviors. They would want the Allies to be rescuers. They would want the Allies to intervene and prevent any other Greater Community force from having access to your world. And people will feel, perhaps, like they have been betrayed or let down because the Allies are not here to protect humanity. But think about this. If the Allies were here to protect humanity, they would have to continue to protect humanity, which would require them, in effect, to take control of your world. All governments in your world would then have to be coordinated with the activities of the Allies. This then would lead to your loss of freedom, even loss of freedom to a friend.

If you want someone to save you, you will give them your power to do so. The Allies will not accept this.

It is not the Allies' purpose to circumvent human authority. It is not their purpose to change governments or allegiances between nations. Their purpose is only to observe the Intervention and to deliver their commentaries. If you want someone to save you, you will give them your power to do so. The Allies will not accept this. And even if they mounted a force necessary to eject the visitors who are interfering in human affairs, to end the Intervention, well, you would have warfare at your borders. And even the Allies' home worlds would be threatened because they are here without any official permission from other worlds or from trading unions or anything like this. What we mean by this is that the Allies are really not supposed to be here doing what they are doing. If you think about this, you will understand. Even in your world, your governments have secret agents trying to get information, trying to intervene in certain ways, either for good or for ill.

The only thing that is going to save humanity is humanity itself. And for this to be possible, humanity must have a greater understanding and take a very sober and objective approach to life in the Universe. As it is now, generally speaking, most people take a very romantic view of life in the Universe. They are dazzled by technology and want more. They think "contact" will bring them untold benefits. They think that advanced nations will teach humanity how to live in peace, how to maintain the environment and how to elevate the standard of living for people everywhere.

> The only thing that is going to save humanity is humanity itself.

Think about this. Is this possible? Do you think people want to have their lives changed and controlled by unknown forces? The visitors may promise these things because it feeds right into people's expectations and desires. The visitors tell people, "Oh, of course, we will give you peace and equanimity. We have no war." Do you wish to give over the authority of your life and have your life and circumstances completely controlled for a mere promise of greater technology or a promise of peace and equanimity in the world? There is peace in the prison because everyone is controlled. But is this really peace? Or is this simply the restraint of war?

Then there are people in the world whose financial positions will be threatened by the Intervention, and they will either resist the Intervention to protect their wealth and their privileges, or they will attempt to unite with the Intervention for their own benefit. Their uniting with the Intervention represents a very dangerous scenario, and one must be quite sober and objective to deal with it effectively.

Many people will simply go into denial and say, "Well, this can't possibly be! I don't believe this. Advanced civilizations don't behave like this. And if they are here, they could help us, and we should welcome them!"

And of course there are many people who simply cannot even consider these things because the reality of the Intervention is beyond their range of comprehension entirely. Life in the Universe? Well, fine, maybe at the far ends of the Galaxy, but not here!

And then there will be people who will say, "Oh, these Allies are right! We have to defend ourselves! Let's build bunkers and live underground and store up weapons and mistrust everyone and everything."

So, it is possible that *The Allies Briefings* may create some hysteria. It is certain there will be denial. It is certain they will be condemned and attacked by people from different viewpoints. But this is the risk that must be taken when a vital message is delivered, into your world or into any world.

Can the truth be received here without anxiety and condemnation? Well, look at the history of the great Spiritual Teachers who have become public with their messages. That gives you a very good demonstration. A few people are reached, and many are outraged. There will be outrage over *The Allies*

Briefings, but a few people will be reached, and they will be able to reach other people. And over time, a new understanding and awareness will slowly work its way into the human consciousness. This awareness is vitally important, for humanity is grossly unprepared for the Greater Community, so unprepared, in fact, that the situation has become rather desperate. Something has to be done or humanity will give away the keys to the Kingdom freely, openly, with very little question.

Look at the history of the peoples of your world, the native peoples of the world, those who simply acquiesced and said, "Oh, yes, fine. Welcome. Move on in. We'll live here, and you can live over there, and everything will be fine." Look what happened here. Is this new scenario really very different? It is a very difficult situation to be the race that is discovered, to be the natives of a new world, being visited by others who seek the values and wealth and opportunities of the new world. Such is the predicament that humanity is in now.

> Can the truth be received here without anxiety and condemnation?

Yet is this a great tragedy? It could become a great tragedy, depending on how people respond. However, it is also a great opportunity, for the presence of forces from the Greater Community intervening into human affairs is really the one great chance for humanity to unite itself and to become strong in its own defense. It takes something of this magnitude to overcome the tribal animosities and histories between cultures. It takes something greater, a greater problem, to unite people.

It is like being in a house on fire. If people in one room won't speak to people in another room, and the people upstairs hate the people downstairs, and the house is on fire, well, you either help each other, or you perish! The world is like a house on fire. It is on fire through environmental degradation and through increasing conflicts between nations and cultures. But the greater fire in the world is the presence of the visitors. The greater fire is the Intervention.

Humanity can deal with these other problems though it has not done so sufficiently yet. But can it deal with the presence of those from beyond the world who possess skills that humanity has not yet cultivated? You can clean up your own backyard. You can change the structure of government. You can slowly, with great difficulty, bring greater justice into the world, and indeed this must be done. But can you deal with the reality of intelligent life from beyond your world without romance, without hopeful expectation, without greed? Can you deal with this objectively and honestly? Can you say to the visitors, "All right, if you are here, then you must reveal yourselves and your intentions, and we will determine if you have a right to be here or not!"

As the Allies describe in their Briefings, humanity should not let *any* foreign race upon its soil without permission from the population. Obviously, under current circumstances, this permission was never asked for and never granted. That is why it is an Intervention and not a visitation. Visitors are welcomed in. They have asked permission to visit. They are here on a visit, with the permission of those being visited. But an Intervention does not have this permission. It is

> It is a very difficult situation to be the race that is discovered, to be the natives of a new world.

> The presence of forces from the Greater Community intervening into human affairs is really the one great chance for humanity to unite itself and to become strong in its own defense.

forced upon you. Some people may say, "Perhaps the visitors did ask for permission, and it was denied by the governments of the world." Well, even if this were the case, the visitors should be on their way and not be here. Even if the governments of the world made a mistake in not welcoming the visitation, if it was not welcomed, then the visitors should not be here—unless they came to conquer and to intervene for this purpose.

Why else would they be here and getting so involved in human affairs, taking such great interest in human physiology, psychology and religion? Do you think they are lacking these things and that is why they are visiting? Do you think they are going to steal the books out of your library? They could get all this information simply by being observers and collecting all of your data and information and transmissions and so forth. They would not need to be here interfering in human affairs to learn about you. Some people think, "Well, they need our reproductive abilities. Or they need our spirituality. Or they need our emotions. Or they need our religion." This is all foolishness. This is turning a blind eye to the obvious.

> Can you deal with the reality of intelligent life from beyond your world without romance, without hopeful expectation, without greed?

Why do nations intervene with one another? Think about this. It is no different in the Greater Community. The obvious is being missed. People want to think of it in other ways because it is easier to deal with. For goodness sakes, yes! Some people say, "Oh, they are here because they need our help! They need our blood supplies. Or they need our religion and we will help them and we will feel so good about ourselves and they will be so grateful."

Some people think, "Well, they are here to bring us new technology and help us end pollution." Do you think people and governments would use this new technology in such a way? Nations in the world would step upon each other to have this new technology for superiority and strength because nations are competing with each other.

Some people say, "Well, they are here because they want to study us." Why would they want to study you? They could study you by receiving your transmissions, which are being projected out into space. Your information is very accessible. It does not require them to be here to study you. And why would they want to study you anyway? Why would so much time and effort be spent in studying human beings? Do you think this is a science project? Do you think this is a cultural exploration? Do people think that humanity is *so* fascinating, so marvelous and so remarkable that other races would spend this kind of time studying you?

The only reason that races are studied is for economic or political advantage in the Greater Community. And these races are studied without their permission. Would you want someone to say, "We would like to study you. Would you be our laboratory experiment for the rest of your life? We will try not to harm you." Would you agree to that? Especially if you found out that you were being used in order for your investigators to take advantage of everything you are and everything you have? Many people think, "Well, the visitors are here to help us," but really they are here to help themselves. And people are making it very easy for them to do this.

> The obvious is being missed. People want to think of it in other ways because it is easier to deal with.

So you might ask, "Well, why aren't more people aware of this?" The answer to that is difficult because it deals with several different factors. The first is people's cultural conditioning and religious conditioning that really do not allow for the reality of intelligent life in the Universe, regardless of their perhaps liberal views on the subject. When it comes right down to it, there is no place in human awareness for life in the Universe, unless it is at the level of a primitive life form, of course. A piece of bacteria is fine. An intelligent race intervening in human affairs is not fine.

> Many people think, "Well, the visitors are here to help us," but really they are here to help themselves.

The governments of the world will not reveal what they know because they have no defense. And the defenses they do have they cannot fully employ without notifying the public, and they do not trust the public, their own populations, to support such an effort without going into panic. Would the government of your country publicly announce, "We have an Intervention going on from races beyond the world. We don't really understand their technology. We are not sure of all of their activities. And we have no defense against them"?

People think they should be told, but most people could not handle it. They could not take it in. They would run and try to hide somewhere. They would think the end of the world was at hand.

> The governments of the world will not reveal what they know because they have no defense.

There are people who are aware of the Intervention but say, "Well, we must be very careful not to come to any premature conclusions here. I mean, we have to gather more facts. We need more evidence." Really? For what? Can't you just see this and know this for what it is? Are you going to spend the rest of your life piecing it together in little tiny pieces? This is not a science experiment. This is the interaction between life forms!

People think they should be told, but most people could not handle it.

If you were diagnosed with a serious illness, would you want to become part of a laboratory experiment? Or would you want to get cured? You would likely want a path of healing established as soon as possible, and if you were sincere about relieving yourself of your illness, you would give it all of your attention. But certain people treat the Intervention as if it were a science experiment, and they are going to take a very long time and piece it all together, and they don't want to be wrong. Meanwhile, their world is being undermined right underneath their feet. They don't know it, and they don't see it, and they don't want to come to these conclusions because they seem unscientific, and they seem outrageous, and where is the proof? And what is proof? How much do you have to see before it is clear? Given the clandestine nature of the Intervention, well, not much is being shown to people. Not in broad daylight anyway.

Can't you just see this and know this for what it is?

So, attempting to be scientific, you piece it together, and you are on the path of seeking the truth, and you don't get the truth, and you haven't gotten the truth, and you won't get the truth. And you are ambivalent about getting the truth because if you really see what it is, well, your science experiment is over. And now you must really act! You must really do something! And your colleagues will look at you like you are crazy, like you have lost your mind, like you have given up your reason and objectivity and taken a wild and outrageous position. So, as much as the truth is sought, at least in theory, it is denied, and no one wants to take the risk of knowing anything. This is a very hard thing to come to terms with, by the way. We understand this. This may be the hardest thing you have ever come to terms with, other than your own mortality.

We don't expect people to simply accept this at first notice. But we must address those tendencies, beliefs and attitudes that prevent people from knowing this at any time. You don't want to wait for the proof because then it will be too late. By then, there will be very little recourse.

> As much as the truth is sought, at least in theory, it is denied, and no one wants to take the risk of knowing anything.

Then people will say, "Well, the visitors have really taken over everything now. I guess it means that's why they're here!" And what do you do then? Protest? Write letters to your senator? Complain to your friends? This is a very serious situation. People must take risks here to see and to know. But even in taking risks, you need some help because you cannot see what is beyond your borders.

Could the Native American peoples understand the intricacies and competition between European nations? No, they could not. Not without help from a more mysterious source. And indeed at that time, the Angelic Presence was active in trying to notify the peoples of the Americas that great and tragic changes were coming. But like yourselves, the Natives could not respond because it was outside the realm of their world view. It did not fit with their beliefs or understanding, and so such revelations, to the extent they could be made available to people, were largely rejected or ignored. Do you think that the Angelic Presence just looked the other way and let the Native American peoples be obliterated?

People want things to work out well. They want to be comfortable. And so they do not look, and if they look, they do not see, and if they see, they do not comprehend because of what they want. People do not want war, and, as a result, they deny war until war overtakes them. Instead of eradicating the conflict at the very outset, as soon as the spark is lit, they wait for the fire to reach them, and then they say, "Oh, we have to stop this!"

People ask, "Well, what can we really do?" There is a great deal you can really do. You must begin with awareness. You must have an understanding of what you are dealing with. You must not allow any alien force to set foot on the soil of this world without the express permission from the people of your world. You have these rights. You must exercise them.

> People want things to work out well. They want to be comfortable. And so they do not look, and if they look, they do not see, and if they see, they do not comprehend because of what they want.

Here it is necessary to take a very prosaic view of life in the universe. Look up at the stars. They are physical. This is not the Heavens you are looking at. This is not your heavenly state. Everyone in the Universe, living in physical life, must deal with the rigors of physical life—survival, competition, hardship, deprivation. Technology does not end these requirements and these difficulties. In fact, it can make things even more complicated. It solves some problems and creates others.

You must have an adult view of life in the Universe. If you have an adolescent view, you are not going to understand. And your lack of comprehension could truly be tragic. The awareness must be established. This is the purpose of *The Allies Briefings*—to establish the awareness, not to answer every question, not to give you a complete understanding, but to give you an awareness. Gaining an awareness is being alerted to something. It does not mean all your questions regarding it are answered or even addressed. But it does mean you are aware of something.

The Allies' message is very simple and very short, and in many ways very general because it is here to arouse awareness and to correct misunderstanding. That is its purpose. Beyond this awareness, there must be a development in spiritual understanding, an awareness of the Mental Environment and the willingness to establish greater cooperation between nations and cultures.

This is a worldwide problem. It is not a problem for Americans or British or Chinese. It is a worldwide phenomenon. The Intervention does not prize one race over another, except insofar as one race can help achieve the intentions of those who are intervening. In this, there is much emphasis on America because it is the most powerful, influential nation. But this is a worldwide phenomenon.

You as human beings are being challenged. Your right to be here, your right to be free and self-determined in the Universe, is being challenged. Those who are intervening in human affairs believe that you cannot rule yourselves and that you will destroy the world, and so they feel that it is their right and privilege to intervene. Their attitude is, "Well, these human beings! Look

> You must not allow any alien force to set foot on the soil of this world without the express permission from the people of your world. You have these rights.

> You must have an adult view of life in the Universe. If you have an adolescent view, you are not going to understand.

at them! They are like animals! We will bring order and structure here." And some people will think, "Oh, that is wonderful! Finally, we will have order and structure."

Do you really want order and structure imposed upon you in this way and to this degree? This is not the way that humanity will advance or become elevated. This is not the way humanity will establish cooperation and peace within the world. Do you want to be occupied? Because that is what you are facing. A vast, global occupation. And many people will say, "Well, I just can't deal with this. I have other problems." We say, "What other problems do you have that are more important than this?" Yes, there are other things in everyone's life that must be dealt with and resolved, but not at the expense of this awareness. This is the most important awareness that one can have in life, in this world, at this time.

So, you begin with awareness, and then you must study and learn things about life in the Universe. And where can you learn this? At the university? In church? From your parents? From your friends? From the newspaper? Or a magazine? What teaches you about life in the Universe can be learned in part from human history. The understanding of how the world has evolved, and the forces that have shaped it, and how nations have interacted with each other will teach you a great deal about life in the Universe because it is not different. It is only hap-

The Allies' message is very simple and very short, and in many ways very general because it is here to arouse awareness and to correct misunderstanding.

pening on a much greater scale with many more different influences and participants. You need a very sober view of intelligent life in the universe. And you must understand, counter to what is believed by many today, that technology will not save you. It will only change you. Technology has not saved any race in the Universe. It has only changed them.

Yes, there are nations that can overwhelm and dominate others because of technology. But these invading nations have been changed themselves by technology. Technology actually makes you vulnerable in the Greater Community. If you have technology that no one else has, well, everyone wants what you have now. And how are you going to defend what you have and protect what you have? It is a problem that very wealthy people face even in your world. How are they going to protect their wealth and their privilege? This totally changes their lives, their friends, their priorities, and can indeed make their lives truly miserable, and often does.

The best position in the Greater Community is to be self-sufficient, independent and extremely discreet. This is wisdom on a greater scale. Yet you can understand from human culture and your own history how this can be true and why this is true. Does the person who just won a million dollars go out and tell everybody? Well, things will change if they do. Discretion, discernment. Very important. More important now than ever before.

> Many people will say, "Well, I just can't deal with this. I have other problems." We say, "What other problems do you have that are more important than this?"

> This is the most important awareness that one can have in life, in this world, at this time.

Therefore, a great deal can be learned from your own history. You take an objective view and say, "Well, this is what happens when nations of different capabilities interact."

Yet many people still think, "It's manifest destiny. It must be this way. It's the way it is. And it can't be changed. And it would have happened this way anyway." That is ridiculous! It could have happened in many different ways. It could have gone many different ways. History did not have to turn out the way it did. And there are other people in the world who think, "Well, whatever happens is the right thing to happen." This is even more ridiculous.

> The best position in the Greater Community is to be self-sufficient, independent and extremely discreet.

Yet while much may be learned by studying human history, culture and psychology, there must be new information as well, a new perspective. It is not simply new information you need as much as a larger perspective. If you look at things the way you have always looked at them, you are going to see what you have always seen. And nothing new is going to be revealed. So, to have a new understanding, a new revelation, requires a different perspective. Otherwise, the mind simply protects what it already believes in and fends off or fights off anything that challenges that.

A new spiritual perspective and an understanding of spirituality in the Universe is being provided through The Teaching in Greater Community Spirituality. Instead of receiving this gift from the Creator, some people may say, "Well, this is all coming from one person. He is going to become so rich and powerful!" Ha! We hope he doesn't get destroyed, actually. Is it a blessing to have all of this given through you into the world? Is it really a blessing to be maligned and condemned or even deified by people? We think it is a great burden and a great sacrifice to accept such a responsibility. The best thing you can hope for is anonymity, but you won't have it because sooner or later people will find out. "Well, this person really says that he has something that no one else has," and then everyone goes crazy about it. "How can someone say this! Who does he think he is! He must be cavorting with the devil! And if he is cavorting with the Angels, well, why does he get to be the one and not me?" You see, it is hard to be a messenger.

Yet someone has to do it. And a person needs great assistance or it cannot be done. They must have great self-trust, great confidence in the Creator and great discernment to tell whether they are being correctly or incorrectly guided. Certainly, anyone who is protecting their money or their social standing could not be in such a position without great personal conflict.

Therefore, new information is needed here, a new perspective, a Greater Community perspective. You have to start thinking like someone who lives in a Greater Community and not simply someone who lives in a neighborhood or a town. Perspective can be learned. And when you gain a new perspective, particularly a greater perspective like this, well, you can see and know things that simply were not obvious before. And these things will not be based upon speculation but upon clear observation.

At some point, you will say, "Well, of course no one should be visiting us without our permission!" That becomes obvious. Right now, people never even think to ask that question. "Well, I don't know...." At some point, you become aware that spiritually advanced races do not go around intervening in other people's worlds. They may send messages through observers, like the Allies of Humanity, but they do not intervene. The spiritually advanced in the Universe do not do that, regardless of their cultures, their worlds, their temperaments or their natures because this is wisdom and wisdom is universal. So just because someone can fly in a spacecraft and get here quickly, relatively speaking, to think that they are spiritually advanced, well, that is ignorance. So when you gain a Greater Community perspective, you realize that the Wise do not intervene. The Wise do not come here and change everything.

You have to start thinking like someone who lives in a Greater Community and not simply someone who lives in a neighborhood or a town.

There are circumstances where genetic material will be given to an evolving race, but that is not what is occurring in the world at this time, we can assure you. Humanity has everything it needs to be successful. It does not need advanced technology. It does not need alien genetic material. Anyone who tries to tell you otherwise is either part of the Intervention or is unwittingly supporting it.

Humanity needs a new perspective. But within you, and

within the human race, is the seed of Knowledge, your Spiritual Mind. This Knowledge is ancient and has been with you all along. If you can discover it, it will reveal to you what you need to know and what you need to do. Everyone who is born into the world today is born with the potential for understanding the Greater Community because this is the time when humanity gains contact with life in the Universe, which we call the Greater Community. This understanding is in you already.

If any alien race tells you, "Well, we are here to enhance your genetic code," you must not believe this. It is not true. If you really want to be a laboratory animal, if you really want to be subjected to an occupation, if you think this is what it means to have contact with life in the Universe, then what is going to change your mind? Experiencing the occupation and waking up one day and saying, "My God! I am no longer a free person and I have no recourse"?

> Everyone who is born into the world today is born with the potential for understanding the Greater Community because this is the time when humanity gains contact with life in the Universe.

Is it too audacious to say that this is the most important problem in the world and that God has given an answer and the answer has been given in a teaching? Is it too audacious to say that this is the most important problem in the world and God has given an answer, and the answer is being given through one person? How else would the answer be given? Would it be given to a hundred people? The message would never get beyond them if it did.

When Jesus came, were there a hundred Jesuses, all competing with each other? "Well, my Jesus is the real Jesus, but yours is not!" That is not how revelation is brought to the world because it does not work.

We are beyond the world. We are the Angels. So we can say audacious things and then go somewhere else. We don't have to deal with the repercussions. We just deliver the message and people either go crazy with it or they become illuminated by it. But we're somewhere else. It does not affect us.

However, for the messenger, it is another story. He has to face all of the reaction that will occur. It is not an easy job. Be glad that you are not given this job. But understand that as your realization occurs, you will have to advocate for this awareness too. You will not have the difficulty that the messenger has, but you will face all the things that we are talking about. You will see the effects of the Intervention. You will see the effects of the Pacification Program. You will see how listless people are, how critical they are and how much they are in denial. And all of their outrage and all of their suspicion and all of their fear and all of their avoidance, you will see. It will be as clear as day. And you will understand then how revelation occurs in the world. When the message has to be given and time is of the essence, this is how it occurs. This is the difficulty. This is the challenge.

> We just deliver the message and people either go crazy with it or they become illuminated by it.

The real problem ultimately is not with the Intervention, though that is a real problem. The bigger problem is human response-ability. The ability of people to respond. The lack of response. The ignorant response. The negative response. If people cannot respond, well, the world will be given away.

There are not many visitors here in the world. Their numbers are not that great. But their job is being made easy because of human acquiescence and human ignorance. Again, the response. The ability to respond. Response-ability. If there is no response-ability, well, people will not respond, and the occupation will happen, right beneath their feet. And people will think, "Oh, well, something is going on in the world. Things certainly are changing!" And it will seem to be okay until they find out what it really is.

That is why at this time an urgent message is being delivered. The awareness is the first thing. Then you must learn about life in the Greater Community, which you can begin to do by looking at your own world objectively. Then you must begin to gain a Greater Community perspective and learn about life and spirituality in the Universe. This is now being presented in the teaching on Greater Community Spirituality. Not everyone will be able to learn this teaching, but enough people in many places will need access to it in order to comprehend what is going on.

Humanity could end the Intervention tomorrow if it were informed and aware. Humanity could prevent a future Intervention of this kind if it were informed and aware and united. People are so preoccupied with themselves that their borders are undefended. Oh, yes, they have borders, between each other, tremendous borders, walls and resistance and hostility. But your borders to space are undefended. You have no walls to prevent the outside from coming in because you do not think there is an outside that can come in or that will come in.

This, then, is a time for courage, trust and honesty. Time for a real reckoning within yourself. Read *The Allies Briefings* and

> The real problem ultimately is not with the Intervention, though that is a real problem. The bigger problem is human response-ability. The ability of people to respond.

ask yourself, "What do I really know?" not "What do I want?" or "What do I prefer?" or "What do I believe?" but "What do I really know here? Is this really happening?" Consult Knowledge within yourself if you can, not your ideas or your fears or your beliefs, but something deeper within you. That is where the real confirmation will happen. And it will take great courage to ask this because this awareness will change your life. It will set you free. And it will give you direction. But you must be willing to have this change within yourself. This is the revelation that happens within each person. It is much resisted. Much delayed. But if it can take place, it is the most valuable thing.

We send our blessings to you and ask that you receive this counsel and consider it for yourself, for you must make the ultimate decision. We can only inform. We cannot control. The Presence of the Teachers is with you.

MESSAGE FROM
MARSHALL VIAN SUMMERS

As the recipient of *The Allies of Humanity Briefings,* I know what it means to be offered a vision and an understanding greater than one's own. It can be at once overwhelming, enlightening and confusing as it contrasts with so much of what we already assume and believe. I now see that we must pass beyond the threshold of our human isolation into a far greater panorama of life where we as human beings, standing upon our one precious world, are but a small, frail thread within the larger fabric of life in the Universe.

The gift of *The Allies of Humanity Briefings* is twofold. The first gift is to warn us of an impending danger that we are now facing, and the second is to prepare humanity for the greater life that is awaiting us. This requires that we begin to think and act like we are part of a Greater Community of intelligent life and not just a member of one nation, tribe, religion or elite group. This requires that we learn about both the realities of life and the meaning of our spirituality within this Greater Community. *The Allies Briefings* and The Teaching in Greater Community Spirituality are here to reveal these things to us.

Life is moving us forward rapidly and forcing us to face certain realities we have never had to face before. The Greater Community is a new reality. Do we move forward to face this, or do we stay behind with our fears, prejudices and the false security of our old assumptions? We can no longer take a passive approach and wait for our government and religious leaders to guide us in these matters. They may know less than we do, or their position may be compromised by what they don't want us to know. Therefore, *The Allies of Humanity Briefings* are being sent directly to the people. This is where the real power must reside. The fate and future of humanity are now in our hands, each one of us. The Creator has given us the power to meet this and every other challenge and opportunity that life places before us. This power is contained in a deeper intelligence that we all possess, a Knowledge deeper than our intellect, our beliefs or our assumptions. Recall for a moment the times in which you inexplicably *knew* something. This is the kind of Knowledge that I am talking about. This is the Knowledge that the Allies are talking about.

The real question before us then is, are we big enough to accept the power and responsibility of such direct knowing? Can we see the truth, hear the truth, recognize the truth and have the courage to act upon the truth? Do we want to be forever lost in our endless conflicts and controversies? Time is running out. We must pass beyond the threshold of our isolation in order to see and to be prepared for the coming of the Greater Community and all that it means. The preparation doesn't start with our leaders doing something. It starts with you and me and the next person who is fortunate enough to receive this new understanding from the Allies of Humanity.

The perspective that we need is now here. Take this new awareness of life in the Universe and share it with others. Allow this new awareness to shed light on the meaning and purpose of your life in the world at this time. Be a part of the growing movement of people who are beginning to respond to the Greater Community. The calling is here. It is time to respond.

THERE IS A NEW HOPE
IN THE WORLD

Hope in the world is rekindled by those who become strong with Knowledge. Hope can fade away and then be reignited. It can seem to come and go, depending on how people are swayed and what they choose for themselves. Hope rests with you. Because the Unseen Ones are here does not mean that there is hope, for without you, there would be no hope. For you and others like you are bringing a new hope into the world because you are learning to receive the gift of Knowledge. This brings a new hope into the world. Perhaps you cannot see this fully at this moment. Perhaps it seems beyond your understanding. But from a greater perspective, it is so very true and so very important.

The world's emergence into the Greater

Community speaks to this, for if no one were preparing for the Greater Community, if no one were learning The Greater Community Way of Knowledge or Greater Community Spirituality, then hope would seem to fade. And humanity's destiny would seem to be utterly predictable. But because there is hope in the world, because there is hope in you and in others like you who are responding to a greater calling, the destiny of humanity has greater promise, and the freedom of humanity may well yet be secured.

◆

FROM *STEPS TO KNOWLEDGE*

Resistance

&

Empowerment

◆

RESISTANCE & EMPOWERMENT

Taking Action — What you can do

◆

At every turn, the Allies encourage us to take an active role in discerning and opposing the extraterrestrial Intervention that is occurring in our world today and in the process begin to build the human freedom, cooperation and unity that can assure our freedom and future in the Greater Community. We have the power to do this. It is up to us.

To offset the Intervention and to achieve this unity will ultimately require skill, commitment and cooperation from people of many different disciplines, cultures and faith traditions. It all begins with awareness. Therefore, our first task is to bring this new awareness of the Greater Community and the message of *The Allies Briefings* to as many people as possible. There are four things that everyone can do *right now*:

- DEVELOP YOUR OWN AWARENESS. Do not let your everyday life overshadow your awareness of this grave situation. Study and reread the Allies Briefings. Explore the questions that they provoke. See the Intervention for what it is, see its greater implications and see how it could affect your life and the future of all the things that you value. Study The Way of Knowledge. This is how the Allies gained their strength and wisdom. They are students of Knowledge.

• SHARE THE ALLIES' MESSAGE WITH OTHERS. Your friends and family (and even enemies) need to hear this message. Your government, business and religious leaders need to hear this message. Spread this new awareness. Share this new perspective. Be alert for opportunities to advocate. This information must be shared as widely as possible. Everyone has the potential to see the truth about the Intervention, but they may never see it if no one shows them. In this way, this vital message can spread quickly and effectively through many human networks.

• SUPPORT HUMAN UNITY AND SOVEREIGNTY IN OUR WORLD. Use the presence of the Intervention as a rallying cry for human cooperation and unity. Speak out against national, cultural and religious conflict in any form. No nation or group will be victorious if the entire world is lost. It is time to strengthen the human family. As The Allies Briefings tell us, a divided humanity will have no power or efficacy in the Greater Community.

• SUPPORT THE WORK OF MV SUMMERS AND THE SOCIETY FOR THE GREATER COMMUNITY WAY OF KNOWLEDGE who have been given The Allies Briefings and are the first to champion this great cause. There are six billion people to reach with the Allies Message and The Teaching in Greater Community Spirituality. Your financial contribution is urgently needed to make possible the worldwide dissemination of this critical message in order to turn the tide for humanity. Visit The Society's website at: www. newmessage.org.

We stand now at a great threshold. Your participation and contribution are critical to the success of this great cause. No one else is going to do this work for humanity. It is up to us and to others like us to support this cause and to begin to build this new awareness throughout the human family. As in all great causes, it begins with inspired individuals and small groups of people responding to a great need. And surely this is the greatest need of all.

TEN-POINT SUMMARY OF THE ALLIES OF HUMANITY BRIEFINGS
BOOK ONE & BOOK TWO

To assist you in sharing the Allies' Message with others, we are including this ten-point summary of both sets of the Briefings. This summary represents only a general overview and does not include many of the important details that make a complete comprehension of the Allies Briefings possible. Visit www.alliesofhumanity.org for a downloadable version to share with others.

1. Humanity's destiny is to emerge into and to engage with a Greater Community of intelligent life in the Universe.

2. Contact with other forms of intelligent life represents the greatest threshold that humanity has ever faced. The results of this Contact will determine humanity's future for generations to come. This Contact is happening now.

3. Humanity is unprepared for Contact. Researchers are still unable to clearly see who is visiting our world and why. Governments are not revealing what they know, and most people are still in denial that this phenomenon is even occurring.

4. Because of this lack of preparation, humanity's true allies sent representatives to a location near Earth to observe the extraterrestrial presence and activities within our world. *The Allies of Humanity Briefings* represent their report.

5. The Briefings reveal that our world is undergoing an extraterrestrial Intervention by forces that, as demonstrated by their actions, are here to subvert human authority and to integrate into human societies for their own advantage. These forces represent non-military organizations that are here to seek human and biological resources. The Allies refer to these forces as the "Collectives." The Collectives do not value human freedom.

6. Because the Intervention is being carried out by small groups of intervening forces, it must rely primarily upon deception and persuasion to achieve its goals. *The Allies Briefings* describe in detail how this is being accomplished and what we must do to stop it.

7. This extraterrestrial Intervention is being focused in four arenas:

    • It is influencing individuals in positions of power and authority to cooperate with the Intervention through the promise of greater wealth, power & technology.

    • It is creating hidden establishments in the world from which the Intervention can exert its influence in the Mental Environment, seeking to make people everywhere open and compliant to its will through a "Pacification Program."

    • It is manipulating our religious values and impulses in order to gain human allegiance to its cause.

- It is taking people against their will, and often without their awareness, to support an interbreeding program designed to create a hybrid race and a new leadership who would be bonded to the "visitors."

8. Those extraterrestrial visitors who have been potentially beneficial to humanity have all retreated from the world in the face of the Intervention. Those remaining are alien races who are not here for our benefit. This leaves us in an unambiguous situation regarding the extraterrestrial presence. This enables us to clearly see what we are dealing with. Otherwise, it would be impossible for us to tell friend from foe.

9. *The Allies Briefings* emphasize the grave danger in our accepting and becoming reliant upon ET technology offered by the Intervention. This will only lead to our becoming dependent on the "visitors," resulting in our loss of freedom and self-sufficiency. No true ally of humanity would offer this to us. The Allies emphasize that we have Earth-based solutions to all the problems that we face. What we lack as a race are unity, will and cooperation.

10. In spite of the great challenge we now face, humanity still has a great advantage if we can respond in time. *The Allies Briefings* reveal both the Intervention's strengths and its weaknesses. One of the Intervention's weaknesses is its reliance upon human acquiescence and cooperation to achieve its goals. According to Greater Community rules of conduct within the region in which our world exists, Intervention is not allowed unless it can be demonstrated that the native people welcome and approve of it. Here, our voices can have power

in the Greater Community. At this moment the Intervention has few critics. But if enough people can become aware of it and speak out against it, the Intervention will be thwarted and must withdraw. This is the first step in humanity's preparation for dealing with the realities of life in the Universe. This step and all the steps that follow give humanity its one great chance to overcome its long-standing conflicts and to unite in its own defense for the preservation of the world. The Allies affirm that we as human beings have the spiritual and collective power to do this and that we must do this if we want to survive and advance as a free and independent race in the Greater Community.

◆

"*If humanity were well versed in Greater Community affairs, you would resist any visitation to your world unless a mutual agreement had been established previously. You would know enough not to allow your world to be so vulnerable.*"

THE ALLIES OF HUMANITY, BOOK ONE
THE FOURTH BRIEFING

Appendix

◆

DEFINITION OF TERMS

THE ALLIES OF HUMANITY: A small group of physical beings from the Greater Community who were hidden in the vicinity of our world in our Solar System. Their mission was to observe, report and advise us on the activities of the alien visitors and Intervention in the world today. They represent the Wise in many worlds.

THE VISITORS: Several other alien races from the Greater Community "visiting" our world without our permission who are actively interfering in human affairs. The visitors are involved in a long process of integrating themselves into the fabric and soul of human life for the purpose of gaining control of the world's resources and people.

THE INTERVENTION: The alien visitors' presence, purpose and activities in the world.

THE PACIFICATION PROGRAM: The visitors' program of persuasion and influence aimed at disarming people's awareness and discernment of the Intervention in order to render humanity passive and compliant.

THE GREATER COMMUNITY: Space. The vast physical and spiritual Universe into which humanity is emerging which contains intelligent life in countless manifestations.

THE UNSEEN ONES: The Angels of the Creator who oversee the spiritual development of sentient beings throughout the Greater Community. The Allies refer to them as "The Unseen Ones." In the Teaching on Greater Community Spirituality, they are also referred to as the "Teachers of the Greater Community."

HUMAN DESTINY: Humanity is destined to emerge into the Greater Community. This is our evolution.

THE COLLECTIVES: Complex, hierarchical organizations composed of several alien races which are bound together by a common allegiance. There is more than one Collective present in the world today to which the alien visitors belong. These Collectives have competing agendas.

THE MENTAL ENVIRONMENT: The environment of thought where more concentrated minds exert mental influence and persuasion on weaker minds.

KNOWLEDGE: The spiritual intelligence that lives within each person. The source of all that we know. Intrinsic understanding. Eternal Wisdom. The timeless part of us which cannot be influenced, manipulated or corrupted. A potential in all intelligent life. Knowledge is God in you and God is all Knowledge in the Universe.

THE WAY OF KNOWLEDGE: Various teachings in learning Knowledge and Wisdom that are taught in many worlds in the Greater Community.

GREATER COMMUNITY SPIRITUALITY: A spiritual teaching from the Creator that is practiced in many places in the Greater Community. It teaches how to experience and express Knowledge and how to preserve individual freedom in the Universe. This teaching has been sent here to prepare humanity for the realities of life in the Greater Community.

ABOUT THE AUTHOR

Though he remains little known in the world today, Marshall Vian Summers may ultimately be recognized as the most significant spiritual teacher to emerge in our lifetime. For more than twenty years, he has been quietly writing and teaching a spirituality that acknowledges the undeniable reality that humanity lives in a vast and populated universe and now urgently needs to prepare for the challenge of emerging into a Greater Community of intelligent life.

MV Summers teaches the timeless Knowledge and Wisdom from the Greater Community that is so needed in the world today if humanity is to overcome conflict and inequality and prepare for the Greater Community. His books *Greater Community Spirituality: A New Revelation* and *Steps to Knowledge: The Book of Inner Knowing*, winner of the Year 2000 Book of the Year Award for Spirituality, together present a new spiritual paradigm that could be considered the first "Theology of Contact." Of the entire body of his work, some twenty volumes, only a handful have yet been published by New Knowledge Library. These works together represent some of the most original and advanced spiritual teachings to appear in modern history.

Marshall is the Founder of The Society for The Greater Community Way of Knowledge, a non-profit organization dedicated to bringing into the world a new awareness of humanity's place in the Universe. With *The Allies of Humanity: Books One & Two*, Marshall becomes perhaps the first major spiritual teacher to sound a clear warning about the real nature of the extraterrestrial Intervention now occurring in the world, calling for personal responsibility, preparation and collective awareness. He has devoted his life to receiving The Teaching in Greater Community Spirituality, a gift to humanity from the Creator. He is committed to sharing this "New Message" from God with as many people as possible.

ABOUT THE SOCIETY

The Society for The Greater Community Way of Knowledge has a great mission in the world. The Allies of Humanity have presented the reality of the Intervention and the need for humanity to prepare for its future in the Greater Community. In response to this immense challenge, a preparation has been given in The Teaching in Greater Community Spirituality. The Teaching provides the Greater Community perspective and a unique method of preparation that people from all faith traditions and walks of life can use to discover Knowledge, their deeper spiritual intelligence, and to prepare for a future that will be unlike anything that we have ever known. It is this innate Knowledge that the Allies of Humanity are urging us to use for our self-protection and advancement as a race.

The Society was founded as a non-profit 501 (3) (C) religious organization in 1993 by Marshall Vian Summers and a group of dedicated people. The mission of The Society is to receive and to present The Teaching in Greater Community Spirituality worldwide. *The Allies of Humanity Briefings* represent a unique part of this Teaching.

The work of The Society is to present Greater

Community Spirituality through its publications, websites, educational programs and contemplative services and retreats. It is through our work that we endeavor to inspire human cooperation, human unity and human advancement. Join with us in supporting this great mission. Contact The Society if you would like to make a tax-deductible contribution to this great work that can truly change the course of our future.

"*Greater Community Spirituality is being presented into the world,*

where it is unknown.

It comes in a naked form—without ritual and pageantry,

without wealth and excess.

It comes purely and simply.

It is like a child in the world.

It is seemingly vulnerable, and yet it represents

a greater reality and a greater promise for humanity."

THE TEACHERS OF THE GREATER COMMUNITY

THE SOCIETY FOR
THE GREATER COMMUNITY WAY OF KNOWLEDGE

P.O. Box 1724, Boulder, CO 80306-1724
(303) 938-8401, fax (303) 938-1214
society@greatercommunity.org
www.newmessage.org

THE WRITINGS OF
MV SUMMERS

THE ALLIES OF HUMANITY, BOOK ONE: An Urgent Message About the Extraterrestrial Presence in the World Today. The first set of Briefings. Reveals the four fundamental activities of the Intervention. This message speaks to the many people who feel a connection between the ET reality and spirituality. It provides new information and a Greater Community perspective on the alien Intervention, its challenges  and its opportunities for humanity at this great turning point.

ISBN 978-1-884238-45-1: Six Briefings,186 pages:

Trade Paper: $14.95

GREATER COMMUNITY SPIRITUALITY: A New Revelation. Provides new answers to 27 fundamental questions about the meaning of life, our relationship with God and our destiny, all from a Greater Community perspective. The "Theology of Contact" for understanding the reality and the spirituality of intelligent life in the universe.

ISBN 978-1-884238-50-5: 27 chapters, 390 pages:

Trade Paper: $17.95

STEPS TO KNOWLEDGE: The Book of Inner Knowing. A profound guide to experiencing and applying Knowledge, the greater Spiritual Intelligence that lives within you. The preparation book for humanity's emergence into a Greater Community of intelligent life. The Book of Practices in Greater Community Spirituality. Winner of the "Year 2000 Book of the Year Award" for Spirituality.

ISBN 978-1-884238-27-7: 365 practices, 524 pages: Trade Paper: $25

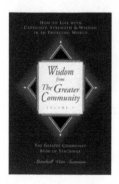

WISDOM FROM THE GREATER COMMUNITY, Volume I: How to Live with Certainty, Strength and Wisdom in an Emerging World. The Greater Community Teaching on topics ranging from "Marriage" and "Achieving Peace" to "Provoking Change" and "World Evolution." 35 Chapters. The First Book of Discourses in Greater Community Spirituality.

ISBN 978-1-884238-28-4: 35 chapters, 452 pages: Trade Paper: $25.

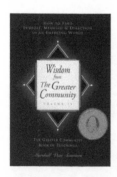

WISDOM FROM THE GREATER COMMUNITY, Volume II: How to Find Purpose, Meaning and Direction in an Emerging World. The Greater Community Teaching on topics ranging from "Discernment" and "Solving Problems" to "Environments" and "Visitors' Perceptions of Humanity." 34 Chapters. The Second Book of Discourses in Greater Community Spirituality. Silver Award Finalist in the 1997 Benjamin Franklin Book Award for Spirituality.

ISBN 978-1-884238-29-1: 34 chapters, 452 pages: Trade Paper: $25.

LIVING THE WAY OF KNOWLEDGE: Building the Foundation for Becoming a Man or Woman of Knowledge in an Emerging World. How to bring the grace, the guidance and the power of Knowledge into the "Four Pillars" of your life: your relationships, your work, your health and your spiritual direction. After *STEPS TO KNOWLEDGE,* the second great practice for learning and living The Way of Knowledge.

ISBN 978-1-884238-03-1: 11 chapters, 168 Pages: Wire Bound: $20.

Currently available only through New Knowledge Library.

RELATIONSHIPS & HIGHER PURPOSE: Finding Your People, Your Purpose and Your Mission in the World. A lifelong resource for discovering and fulfilling your true purpose for coming into the world. Reveals the source of each person's deep yearning for true relationship and offers a revolutionary understanding of those key relationships that will change your life. Not merely a book to read, but a companion book meant to be studied, deeply considered and applied.

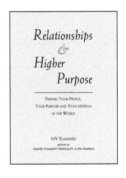

ISBN 978-1-884238-87-1: 15 chapters, 192 Pages: Wire Bound: $30.

Currently available only through New Knowledge Library.

The Books of The Greater Community Way of Knowledge can be requested at your local bookstore or ordered from amazon.com. You can also order directly from us at New Knowledge Library. At this time LIVING THE WAY OF KNOWLEDGE and RELATIONSHIPS & HIGHER PURPOSE are not available in bookstores and can be ordered only from New Knowledge Library at nkl@greatercommunity.org or (303) 938-8401. For book orders outside of Colorado please call 1-800-938-3891. To view the Books of Knowledge in greater detail, please visit our website at www.newmessage.org.